Self-Centered Co-Parenting™
Managing the Uncooperative Co-Parent

By Kathleen Bird, JD

Book cover by Alma Lafler

ISBN: 9978-0-9987321-1-4

Library of Congress Control Number: 2017903736
New Notion Publications, Liberty, MO

Table of Contents

INTRODUCTION

Why Self-Centered Co-Parenting?
Your child deserves effective parenting.

Parenting with a co-parent who lives separately is a challenge. There are many tasks to coordinate while raising your child. Timely and effective communication is an on-going chore. Advice books on co-parenting often assume that both parents are willing to cooperate. Unfortunately, as many as half the co-parents living separately find that getting cooperation is a major problem. The experience of these frustrated parents may sound familiar.

"Co-parenting? That's rich! There is no cooperation at all. Whenever I try to arrange something I can never get a timely answer. If there is any response at all, it is usually a personal attack or a flood of cursing. I've decided that the co-parent is a mental case."

"I am so frustrated that I can never get things arranged for my child. The other parent stonewalls me and refuses to return calls or reply to email. But when the co-parent wants something, I better jump on it quick or there will be trouble."

"I just want to see my kid, but it's blocked at every turn. I know the co-parent is saying things to our child that makes him hate me and refuse to see me. Why is the co-parent allowed to get away with this?"

"Our court order is just a piece of paper. Why can't a judge make the other parent do right? There should be some way to enforce our parenting orders. The system is letting the co-parent get away with games that harm our child."

The conventional co-parenting advice that urges you to *"just get along"* isn't working. It takes two to cooperate, but it only takes one parent to undermine effective parenting by refusing to cooperate. A lot of time and effort is put into finding ways to make the co-parent do the right thing. Many frustrated parents turn to lawyers and court in hopes of invoking authority that will make the co-parent behave. Parents can get caught in a revolving door at the courthouse as they engage in repeated attempts to make changes or seek sanctions in hopes of improving things. Unfortunately, changes in custody and decision-making terms don't entirely fix the problem because the parents still have to continue to interact with each other in so many ways that can't be supervised on a day-to-day basis by a court.

Your situation can be improved despite the co-parent's lack of interest in cooperating. There is no advantage to waiting in hopes that the co-parent will change. The co-parent will only change when and if the other parent wants to change. For reasons explained in this book, trying to force a co-parent to cooperate often has the opposite effect. You can become more effective in handling an uncooperative co-parent right now by using what is already in your own control . . . YOU. Your thoughts, your words and actions, when used strategically and effectively, have the power to change interactions with the co-parent for the better. You have the power to take the steps that can make this happen.

This book discusses five strategies for Self-centered co-parenting that give you the control you need to parent your child with less frustration and conflict. This involves that scary word: c-h-a-n-g-e. If you identify with any of the sentiments expressed by parents above, you know what lack of cooperation is doing to your quality of life and that of your child. More of the same will only get the same result. Change is required. Identifying your underlying fears, concerns, and needs is a crucial first step in planning how to gain control. It will help you identify what needs to change.

Self-Diagnosis
Check all that apply.

☐ I feel shut out of a fulfilling parental role in my child's life.
☐ I am frustrated the co-parent isn't doing their part to raise our child.
☐ Dealing with the co-parent is unpleasant, stressful, even exhausting.
☐ Communication with the co-parent is argumentative and unproductive.
☐ Communication with the co-parent is non-existent.
☐ My child is caught in the middle of parenting power struggles.
☐ My child's right to spent time with me is not honored.
☐ My child's right to communicate with me is not honored.
☐ Decisions are made by chance, with little thought or planning.
☐ I feel hopeless about dealing with problems when they come up.
☐ I tend to avoid a fight or give up rather than address an issue.
☐ I feel I have no choice but to fight.
☐ The lack of cooperation is depleting my time, energy, and money.
☐ The lack of control over this situation is driving me crazy!

If you checked more than a couple of boxes, the situation is hard on you and dangerous for your child. These are things you will want to change.

How lack of cooperation harms a child

When parenting is not coordinated, important tasks start to fall through the cracks: unreturned clothing, school information not shared, homework assignments not turned in, missed activities, missed checkups and dental appointments, and so on. As failures pile up, your child's ability to keep up is diminished. When parental relations are dysfunctional, decisions aren't made that parents would otherwise make in informed and thoughtful ways. The child's well-being is managed by chance instead of intentional decision-making. All children, and especially your child, deserve better.

Fault-finding between parents generates conflict that pulls their child into their arguments. Young children in particular feel they are to blame when their parents are arguing about them. Studies verify that parents significantly underestimate the extent to which children are affected by parental conflict. Exposure to parental conflict increases a child's anxiety substantially. Repeated conflict exposes a child to chronic stress which impacts a child's health and can adversely affect normal child development. Much has been written about the effects of parental conflict on children and none of the consequences are things you want to tolerate for your child. It doesn't have to continue.

Why try self-centered co-parenting?

I have spent nearly four decades working with parents who are frustrated and angry about the lack of cooperation from their child's co-parent. After a lot of thought, research, and experience I have arrived at an important conclusion: forcing, mandating, and punishing uncooperative and misbehaving co-parents has fleeting success at best. The effort to force a co-parent to toe the line is very costly and exhausting for the minimal and short-lived results that are normally achieved. There must be a way for parents living separately to engage in child-focused and thoughtful parenting regardless of the amount of cooperation between them.

No one cares more about your quality of life or your child's welfare more than you do. You will feel more successful as a parent if you can expend your time and resources on nurturing your child. Self-centered co-parenting is a method for empowering yourself to change the situation in ways that benefit you and your child. Stop trying to change the co-parent and concentrate on what is in your own control.

Learn to harness the tools in your control to make a difference. Focusing on empowering yourself will increase your confidence that you are improving the quality of parenting your child receives regardless of what the co-parent does or doesn't do. First and foremost, you need to build a strong and positive relationship with your child. You are probably wondering how this gets the co-parent to cooperate. We'll get into that, but first here is what we mean by "self-centered co-parenting."

Self-Centered Co-Parenting™
A child-centered way of raising your child with a co-parent who lives independently, by focusing your thoughts, decisions, and actions on things within your own control instead of trying to control the other parent.

Self-centered means being in control of your own thought process, ready to make thoughtful positive choices instead of merely reacting, and taking effective action when necessary to benefit your child. Paying more attention to parenting and less to conflict with the co-parent gives you breathing room to strengthen your relationship with your child and be the kind of parent that you really find fulfilling.

Embrace the five hallmarks of Self-Centered Co-Parenting described below. Each one refers to material in this book. You can quickly access and put the tips in each chapter into play. I encourage you to read more about the concepts behind these tips and why they work. The more thoroughly you understand the concepts the more effective you are going to be in taking control in a productive and successful way.

The Five Strategies of Self-Centered Co-Parenting

1. I will have a genuine, loving and supportive relationship with my child, regardless of what the other parent does or says.

2. I will identify the difference between what I feel like doing in reaction to the co-parent and what I need to do for my child.

3. I will make the best decision I can under the circumstances that are within my control and in the best interest of my child.

4. I commit to interact with the co-parent in a positive and constructive manner that relieves stress and empowers me to do my best parenting.

5. I will take the initiative, when necessary, to manage disputes effectively in order to further the best interests of my child.

Sounds like a big job, doesn't it? But doesn't this also sound like the type of parenting your child deserves? These five strategies embrace the attitudes and skills that you can model to show your child how to grow into a confident and mature adult.

If you are looking for advice on ways to break the co-parent or drive a wedge between your child and the co-parent, this is not the book for you. Even if you could pull that off, it does nothing to accomplish your own parenting goals with your child. Those feelings are understandable but not empowering. As Mark Twain said, "the only thing common about common sense is it's not that common." Use this opportunity to reconsider what you think you know and ask yourself how that has been working for you.

How does this make the co-parent cooperate?

Becoming a self-centered co-parent will help you gain positive influence over the other parent. This is an astonishing statement but over and over parents who use these strategies find this to be true. This is a process and you won't see results overnight. Self-centered co-parenting strategies can knock down the barriers that decrease cooperation. When you change the dynamics of parenting interactions, the co-parent cannot continue to function in the same old way. Patience and determination are required to turn the corner and see results. More patience and determination will be required in the future to hold on to whatever cooperation you secure.

Strong emotions can quickly derail co-parents' intention to make good decisions. After some unpleasant experiences, frustrated parents gradually engage in increasingly negative thinking. Negativity affects assumptions about what is happening and the motivations of the other parent. As negativity increases over time, a parent is even more inclined to think the worst of the other parent's values and behaviors. Judging and blaming each other becomes routine. The other parent's failings are emphasized, with little incentive to remember their strengths and good qualities.

Negative reactivity prompts us to assume the worst rather than keep an open mind until the situation can be assessed accurately. Communications between parents become more judgmental and lead to threats and ultimatums. The response to this is more defensive and argumentative communications. On the other hand, a parent who is uncomfortable with confrontation may tune out and refuse to engage altogether. The downward spiral of negativity causes resentment on both sides. There is bitterness about disrespectful treatment, unfairness, and foul play. Even when interactions are undertaken in hope of reaching a decision, the negative dynamics quickly cause parents to lose hope that an agreement can ever be reached. Parents then resort to costly power plays, such as litigation, to gain control. Even if control is achieved this way, it is generally temporary. It only lasting as long as the circumstances which enabled the power play remain in effect. "Victories" are usually fleeting. The cycle repeats itself over and over again.

Look at all the negative aspects of uncooperative co-parenting we have just discussed: negativity, reactivity, unsupported assumptions, blaming, demands, defensiveness, arguments, disrespect, loss of hope, one-sided power plays. No wonder there is frustration and loss of interest in re-engaging in an effective way. If this doesn't work, however, why do more of the same?

Give up on focusing on the negative, dysfunctional and destructive behaviors as solutions and see them for what they are: symptoms of what isn't working. Concentrate on constructive and effective conflict management instead of reinforcing the dysfunctional. It only takes one parent to decide to change. A self-centered co-parent has access to strategies that fulfill the desire for a positive and fulfilling parenting role, regardless of the behaviors and responses of the co-parent. When you interact with the co-parent using the skills we discuss, the co-parent often starts to take notice and respond in a more positive manner. I have seen this transformation over and over again. Even if the co-parent doesn't change at all, however, you have accomplished your desire to have the type of relationship with your child and be the type of parent you want to be. The five strategies of Self-Centered Co-Parenting put you on the path to reach your goal.

We invite your skepticism and suggest you give it a shot. These strategies have worked for many other parents who were once as frustrated as you. Self-centered co-parenting will seem taxing, even awkward at first. As you embrace the five strategies discussed in Chapter One through Chapter Five, it gets easier and easier to implement them until they seem to come naturally. Each chapter is written as a how to guide. Take a look at the information referenced in the appendices at the back of the book for background to increase your understanding of the concepts behind the five strategies.

Recommendation for further reading is provided in Appendix 9. Once competency is achieved, you will be able to call on these skills in many ways for the rest of your life.

Best wishes,
The Author

Notes:

The term "co-parent" is commonly used for two people who are biological or legal parents of a child. Referring to someone who frustrates you endlessly as a "co-parent" may seem wrong when little or no co-parenting is taking place. For lack of another suitable and commonly understood term, however, this term will be used to refer to your child's other parent throughout this book.

The five Self-Centered Co-Parenting strategies work well when lack of cooperation is the result of a fractured relationship. You may find it more challenging when mental health or substance abuse is a component of the situation. The self-empowering strategies have some value even when these problems are issues for the co-parent. Please engage in safety planning when on-going domestic violence is present. Exposure to violence is a serious hazard to your child. Use of counseling and support groups are encouraged if that is your situation.

The Five Strategies of
Self-Centered Co-Parenting™

Make it about your child instead of the co-parent.

Chapter 1   I will have a genuine, loving and supportive relationship with my child, regardless of what the other parent does or says.

Chapter 2   I will identify the difference between what I feel like doing in reaction to the co-parent and what I need to do for my child.

Chapter 3   I will make the best decision I can under the circumstances that are within my control and in the best interest of our child.

Chapter 4   I commit to interact with the co-parent in a positive and constructive manner that relieves stress on me and our child, and empowers me to do my best parenting.

Chapter 5   I will take the initiative, when necessary, to manage disputes effectively in order to further the best interests of our child.

CHAPTER 1

Child-Focused Parenting

*Let there be peace in my child's life
and let it begin with me*

The co-parent is the wrong target

A fundamental mistake parents make when they are unable to coordinate their parenting, is to focus on things the other parent should or shouldn't be doing. It can consume all a parent's focus and rob time and attention from parenting the child. Cut back on the energy you are putting into making the co-parent perform or relent. A strong relationship with your child and focusing on your child's needs is a much better use of your time and attention. A major benefit of self-centered co-parenting is the time and space it creates for you to parent instead of chasing after the co-parent.

A strong, positive and supportive relationship with your child is a more effective remedy than targeting the co-parent for blame, domination, punishment. Your child deserves your full attention and best parenting efforts despite the behavior of the other parent. Self-centered co-parenting is about focusing on attending to your child's needs. A self-centered co-parent makes thoughtful decisions about how to accomplish parenting tasks from the viewpoint of what is best for the child.

Reduce the intensity of the co-parenting relationship

An emotionally-charged relationship is the fast lane to disaster when dealing with your child's parent who lives separately. When the brain is emotionally charged, our decisions are reactive instead of deliberate. The rush to fight or flee robs us of the will-power to slow down and think things out. Unmanaged emotions disrupt the informed decision–making process. (*See Appendix 1 – How emotions sabotage problem-solving*).

The best thing you can do for yourself is to change your relationship with the other parent to one that is less intimate and intense. You may not think a relationship with so much negativity is "intimate" but the truth is that love *and* hate are on the most intimate end of the relationship scale. This graph represents the intensity of human relationships.

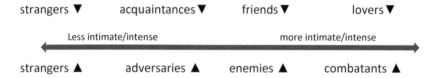

We have no emotional attachment to strangers. We may empathize, based on how we would feel in a similar situation, but we do not form an intimate relationship based on that. We feel somewhat attached to acquaintances and business or social contacts, but the relationship is courteous not intimate. The intensity and intimacy level rises as people become our friends. The most intense and intimate relationship, of course is that of lovers. On the negative side, rivalries share the same end of the scale. When a positive intimate relationship ends, we do not stop having feelings. Because of the value and promise we once saw in the relationship, our feelings remain engaged and flip to the negative. Partners in active combat are as intimately and intensely entwined as people in love. People don't put everything at stake, including their child, in less intense relationships.

When one of you decides the relationship is over, it's healthy to reduce the intensity of the relationship. How far you need to dial back depends on the potential benefits of staying engaged in a positive manner. Some parents living separately do well as friends. They have been able to reduce the intimacy of the relationship over time. Friendship is not comfortable for everyone. If you are in an intense relationship now, it may be best to step back to the role of acquaintances for now. There may be a desire to make your child's other parent a stranger, but that option is not available to you as long as your child is a minor. The parent-child relationship endows your child with legal rights to expect care, support and access to other resources from *both* parents. (*See Appendix 3* – Child's Bill of Rights)

How to reduce intimacy in four steps

You will be able to center yourself and deal with the other parent more effectively once you move to a relationship that focuses on parenting instead of the co-parent. (*See Appendix 4* – Reducing Intimacy)

Step One: Rephrase the on-going role as parent.
Stop thinking of the co-parent in terms of the former role they occupied in your life. That person is no longer your partner or spouse, so don't refer to them as your "ex." Use a neutral term such as co-parent, my child's other parent, etc. The use of a less emotional label will help you think of them in a less intimate way.

Step Two: Understand the extent of your control.
Try to come to terms with the diminished role the other parent plays in your life. The co-parent is now an acquaintance or business contact who is a resource for your child. Try not to put any further expectations on this role. You have no control over that. The other parent will be involved to the extent it makes sense to the other parent.

Step Three: Don't expect any favors.
Since the relationship has changed, the co-parent no longer has to please you. Their only obligations are to the child. From now on, think of all interactions as business transactions.

Step Four: Focus on doing business.
 Avoid social engagement with the co-parent until you feel you can handle it without sparking an emotional reaction.   Limit your interactions for now to those required to conduct business for your child, such as exchanges of the child or meeting at a parent-teacher conference.

Pre-plan the interactions you have with co-parent:

1. Decide what you want to accomplish for your child.

2. Commit to staying focused on your goal for your child.

3. Slow down or take a break if you feel that emotions
     are gaining control and pulling you off task. Don't feel
     compelled to make snap decisions while face to face.

As you depend less on expected performance by the co-parent and start putting your efforts into your own parenting, you should identify what can be accomplished without conditioning it on the cooperation of the co-parent. There are child-focused decisions you can make that are within your own control.

Self-care and presence of mind

To function at peak performance remain aware of what is going on within and around you in a non-judgmental way. Presence of mind allows you to be nimble and open to opportunities instead of stuck in a rut. Stress is empowering when you encounter a physical danger. Day to day, however, stress interferes with the ability to think clearly in the moment.

Become aware of the signs of stress.

Breathing faster	Holding your breath	Talking faster
Chest tightens	Jaw clenched	Talking louder
Face flushes	Making a fist	Teeth clenched
head pounds	Muscles tighten	
Heart races	Palms sweating	

Manage stress by taking a break to center yourself. Slow your thoughts and become aware of your surroundings. Recognize you are not in immediate harm. Of course you want to resolve issues right now, but acting on "gut reactions" may not be the best choice. Concentrate of breathing in and out at a measured pace. Reduce the chances of being hijacked by reactive emotions by getting adequate rest and taking time for reflection. Allow time to engage in an activity you find pleasant and fulfilling. Do not feel guilty about taking this time for yourself. In the long run, this improves your mood for parenting your child. You may think you always need to put your child first, that is not helpful if you are stressed out and not thinking clearly.

Countering badmouthing

A common worry is whether the other parent is doing and saying things to the child to undermine your relationship with the child. This is a bigger problem for the child than it is for you. The child is in a difficult spot when one parent berates the other. By the time a child enters school, most children have developed a sixth sense for a parent's emotional triggers. Children feel inadequate to handle it when someone pulls that trigger and will go out of their way to avoid upsetting the parent. If a child speaks up to defend a parent, the child runs the risk of being called out or punished for being disrespectful. If a child keeps quiet, the child usually feels guilty about being disloyal to the berated parent.

Children should be free to develop their own views about their parents, and as they grow older they will do so regardless of what parents say. By the time children reach puberty there is a keen interest in determining the truth for oneself. To do this a child compares what people say with what people do. Much more credence is given to what people do over what people say. It is sad to put a child in a loyalty bind that will have little effect over time.

Making disparaging comments about a parent is most likely to occur when the relationship remains intimate and intense. Emotions are raw and difficult to manage. A parent who slips into badmouthing mode should find another outlet for their anguish. If you are doing this, find an adult without direct connection to your child, such as a friend or counselor. If the co-parent is doing the badmouthing, hopefully you are starting to realize that you can't make the co-parent stop. Transforming the co-parenting relationship over time to a less intimate level will help.

The best remedy in your own control for badmouthing by the co-parent is to forge a strong and positive relationship with your child. If you do not have any access to your child, you should seriously consider going to court to obtain an enforceable court order that preserves your child's right to have meaningful contact with you. The court order is only the foundation. You will have much work to do to build an enduring relationship with your child. (*See Appendix 2 –* When to Go to Court).

A strong positive relationship with your child

Be a parent who makes your child feel more safe and secure and less responsible for changes in family life.

Envision the best, most rewarding relationship between you and your child. Most parents prefer a relationship that goes well beyond meeting the basic needs of a child for survival. Children crave a solid and loving relationship with both parents. You can certainly hold up your end by meeting your responsibilities, nurturing your child, and reducing the tension that exists between you and the other parent. (*See Appendix 3* – Child's Bill of Rights).

Consider the four components of good parenting:

▶ **Awareness.** A parent knows the stages of child development. A parent is aware of what goes on in the child's world. A parent checks in with teachers, coaches, and other mentors. A parent spends time on the child's turf and knows the people most closely associating with the child.

▶ **Involvement.** A parent participates in the child's life at play, school, activities and unstructured time. A parent reads stories with the child, works on homework and projects, attends events important to the child, and sometimes just hangs out with the child.

▶ **Consistency.** A parent's behavior is predictable. A parent keeps his or her word to the child and does not over-promise. The parent regularly spends time with the child and sees this commitment as necessary for the security of the child rather than the convenience of the parent. A parent focuses on time together as addressing an important need of the child rather than the parent's right to access to the child.

▶ **Encouragement**. A parent responds to the child's emotional needs by expressing affection, encouraging the child to try new things, and praising the child's accomplishments. A parent listens to what the child says as a unique expression of thoughts and feelings the child is entitled to have without judging or diminishing them.

Parenting must include a healthy balance of nurturing and training. A stable parent-child relationship is undermined when a parent feels they must give in or overindulge the child in an effort to win the best parent competition. Resist the urge to let discipline slide. Maintaining your role as the parent in the relationship preserves your child's sense of predictability and security. Active engagement with your child in a positive and compassionate way promotes an emotional connection that makes your child feel safe, heard, and understood. Developing a strong emotional bond and mutual respect encourages your child to likewise develop positive behavior patterns with others. If this is the type of relationship you had with a parent, you already know the skills that were modeled for you. If you did not have a strong positive relationship with a parent, consider counseling to develop positive parenting skills. There are also many commendable books on positive parenting you can use as references.

You have little say, however, over the way the co-parent engages in parenting the child if abuse and neglect are not present. First of all, what is "abuse" or "neglect" is in the eye of the beholder. You may think it is abuse for your child to sleep on the couch during parenting time with the co-parent. You may think it is neglect for the child to only have the option of sugary cereals for breakfast. These are preferences, not fundamental child survival issues. That is the baseline most often used by child protection authorities and the courts. Check out what the baseline is before launching into a campaign to correct or curb the practices of the other parent.

Parents want to secure the best possible quality of life for their child. It's heartrending to realize that your child may not have a co-parent who is pursuing a positive relationship to the same extent as you. As much as you long for your child to have a great relationship with both parents, the only relationship you can control is your own relationship with your child. Concentrating on your own relationship with the child is a much more productive use of your time and resources than worrying about how to make the other parent do better. You have no control over that.

When your child has a problem with the other parent, resist the impulse to assume the role of fixer. Your interference in a relationship you don't control has little chance of reforming the co-parent. The co-parent will likely resent it that you are sticking your nose into the other parent's relationship with the child. A more appropriate role is to work within your own relationship as a "coach" to help your child develop his own plan, as is age appropriate, to engage with the co-parent in constructive ways. Many of the techniques in this book can be modeled in the child's relationship with the parents. Julie Ross and Judy Corcoran dedicated a portion of their book *Joint Custody with A Jerk* to advice on coaching your child when the child has a problem with the other parent. It is well worth reading.

Parenting tasks

As you work to strengthen your relationship with your child also consider the tasks that you can perform alone (self-regulated parenting) and those it is best for both parents to work out (coordinated parenting). The responsibility of the parents to perform some of these tasks may be designated by a court ordered parenting plan. Implementation of coordinated parenting should be your goal if that is required in your court-ordered plan. If the co-parent is highly uncooperative, concentrate on the self-regulated tasks at first. If you detect over time that your self-centered co-parenting skills are having some positive influence over the co-parent, start working on incorporating more of the coordinated tasks into your parenting goals.

CONTACT WITH CHILD	Self-regulated	Coordinated
Phone calls with child		
Mail for child		
Emailing child		
Video chat with child		
Other contact		
CHILD CARE	**Self-regulated**	**Coordinated**
During work hours		
During leisure hours		
When child is ill		
When parent is ill		

FAMILY CELEBRATIONS	Self-regulated	Coordinated
Child's Birthday		
Parent's birthday		
Family reunions		
Visits to extended family		
Other family occasions		

EDUCATION	Self-regulated	Coordinated
School enrollment		
School supplies		
School fees		
School lunches		
School photos		
Homework		
Progress reports		
Teacher conferences		
Tutoring		
PTA activities		
Higher education savings		

HEALTH CARE FOR CHILD	Self-regulated	Coordinated
Maintain health insurance		
Deductibles, co-payments		
Out of pocket expenses		
Scheduling check ups		
Taking child to check ups		
Vaccinations		
OTC medications		
Prescriptions medications		
Maintaining health care records		
Other		

MISCELLANEOUS COSTS	Self-regulated	Coordinated
Activity fees		
Allowance		
Savings account		
Life Insurance		
Other		

LIFE SKILLS & ENRICHMENT	Self-regulated	Coordinated
Activity fees		
Allowance		
Counseling		
Discipline		
Life enrichment activities		
Personal safety training		
Religious training		
Social activities with peers		
Sports activities		
Summer camps		
Volunteer/community service		

NECESSITIES	Self-regulated	Coordinated
Clothing		
Clothing that travels with child		
Dietary needs		
Footwear		
Grooming		
Medications		
Activity equipment		
Activity supplies		
Other		

SECURITY	Self-regulated	Coordinated
Age-appropriate safety seat		
Contact with co-parent		
Child info: school, child care, etc.		
Changes in contact information		
Educate child re address, phone		
Educate child on emergency safety plan		
Emergency contacts		
Other		

TRANSPORTATION	Self-regulated	Coordinated
To School		
To Child Care		
To Activities		
To Healthcare appointments		
To Other Parent's Home		
Other		

Parental alienation

Parental alienation syndrome is a phenomena identified by Robert A. Gardner in the mid 1980's to describe a disorder, usually in context of child custody disputes, where one parent attempts to break off the child's relationship with the other parent. According to Gardner, the syndrome involves repetitive but unjustified denigration of a parent by an alienating parent with of goal of estranging the child from the target parent. Although this theory is popular with parents who think they are the target of alienation, to date the syndrome has not been recognized as a mental disorder by the mental health community. Gardner's research has been criticized for failing to meet prevailing standards for scientific research. The American Psychiatric Association decided not to include the syndrome in its Diagnostic and Statistical Manual of Mental Disorders (the DSM) in 2012. Expert review panels in Great Britain and Canada have rejected the admissibility of the syndrome as evidence in child custody matters. Although parental alienation syndrome has been argued in American courts, it is not universally recognizing as a medical or mental disorder.

Psychologists differentiate "parental alienation" from the diagnosis as a syndrome. A syndrome is considered more severe, and is characterized by the child's hatred and vilification of the targeted parent. At this time the DSM-V does include diagnoses for parental alienation, although the exact terms parental alienation and syndrome are not mentioned. In particular the "parent-child relational problem" and the "child affected by parental relationship distress" are included in DSM-V.

The problems associated with intentional behavior attempting to estrange the child or bar a parent from access to the child are real. This is lack of cooperation run amok. If you are prevented from having contact with your child, it may take the intervention of a court to establish an enforceable schedule of access to the child. Most states recognize the benefits of a specific and regular schedule of parenting time between the child and both parents. Even when there is concern about adequate supervision or a suitable environment for contact between the child and a parent, the court will attempt to set up contact in a manner that protects the safety and security of the child rather than prohibiting contact. Cutting off contact is comparable to termination of parental rights and is only ordered as a last resort.

If you are experiencing estrangement, consider getting help from the court to re-establish the parent-child relationship:

• A specific and detailed parenting schedule, including which parent is responsible for producing the child for exchanges, which parent is responsible for producing the child at the end of parenting time, and terms that require the custodial parent to agree to reasonable requests to rescheduling parenting time.

• Monitored exchanges of the child, preferably with an intermediary who can calm the child between drop off and pick-up. If possible, arrange for documentation of the exchanges that can be made available as evidence in court.

• Use a parenting coordinator, who serves as the facilitator to support both parents in honoring the parenting schedule in a child focused manner. A parenting coordinator addresses issues in real time, whereas action in the court general takes place after the fact and is not as timely.

• Arbitration, as allowed by applicable law, is a process for enforcing parenting time in closer proximity to the infringement than is likely in traditional litigation.

• Counseling between the target parent and the child can help to re-establish or improve the parent child relationship. Counseling for the parent engaging in estrangement may be in order as well to help that parent understand the value of both parents' roles in raising the child.

• A surety bond posted with the court can encourage compliance with the court-ordered schedule. A bond can be forfeited to cover the expenses of the target parent upon on a finding by the court that withholding access was unreasonable under the circumstances.

If you are a targeted parent avoid the temptation to retaliate, seek revenge, or dominate the other parent. Commit to making decisions about contact and interaction with the co-parent that are based on what is best for the child.

Extended Family and Others

The same problem of intense intimacy can exists in parent's relationships with extended family. Be prepared for extended family on both sides to do and say things that are hurtful to the other parent in their inept attempts to demonstrate loyalty to the blood relative. Try not to take it personally. They are also going through emotionally-laden changes. Beware of letting your personal wishes to disconnect deprive your child of their right to have a relationship with the extended family of the other parent. Every person who is connected to your child is a possible resource. Don't interfere with your child's access to extended family solely based on your own feelings about the family members. Try to re-label extended family members in a neutral way. It's likely that things will quiet down over time, especially if you have reduced the intensity of your feelings about them.

Another challenge is the introduction of a new partner. The emotional landscape when step-parents are involved is complex. The parent forming a new attachment has expectations for an intimate relationship with a new partner. A co-parent/former partner may still have feelings about the loss of the old relationship. Unresolved feelings of intimacy may result in attempts to limit the role of the new partner, even competing with the new partner. It may seem right to insist on dealing only with the other parent on the basis that the new partner has no parenting role. But think about it. That person will be spending time with your child when you are not around. Do not create resentment of the child that makes your child's situation in the other parent's household less tolerable.

It is easy to slip into a competitive mode with the new partner of the other parent. The competition is commonly phrased in terms of who has the right to parent and who is butting in. No one wins when the relationship with the new partner is adversarial. A new partner may also be testing the loyalty of the child's parent. If you butt into the newly formed relationship, it will not be well received. Your child is caught in the middle with no way to retreat.

It is best to back away and let the new relationship resolve itself without your involvement. After all, you have no control over how the other parent and new partner interact. If you try to impose your standards or insist on limitations to their roles, you are creating conflict without any power to resolve it. Unless there is a serious issue that fundamentally affects the welfare of the child, you are better off staying away from competition or confrontations with the other parent's new partner. A healthy alliance can develop when the adults focus attention on meeting the needs of the child rather than fighting with each other.

CHAPTER 2
Satisfying Your Needs

Identifying your needs

Life involves decisions about meeting needs and wants. Wants tend to be reflexive desires based on emotion. We can perceive what we *want* to do in the passion of the moment. Needs, on the other hand, are the underlying essentials required to keep us comfortable and secure. American psychologist Abraham Maslow described basic human needs as a pyramid with a base of fundamental needs required for survival building to needs that enrich our lives.

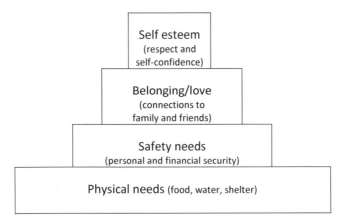

Our wants are the expressed emotional response to a desire to fulfill unexpressed basic human needs. By becoming aware of the emotions connected to our "wants" and identifying the underlying needs, we can work more effectively to satisfy them. Instead of reacting based on our wants, a self-centered co-parent digs below the surface to satisfy the real needs. When basic human needs are satisfied, a self-centered co-parent makes the fullest use of their capacity to become a great parent to the child.

It is important to engage in self-care in order to do the best for your child. For example, if you and your child were on a high-flying aircraft that suddenly lost pressure, would you first put the air masks that drop from the ceiling on yourself or on your child? On an emotional level you would feel compelled to see to your child first. In reality, if a parent does not remain conscious, the parent cannot care for the child. That is why airline attendants direct adult passengers to put their masks on first, and then place the mask on their children. A self-centered co-parent engages in self-care in order recharge and to fill the needs of the child. Commit to reclaiming control over your sense of self in order to feel empowered and confident.

Keep your aspirations reasonable. If the only thing that is going to make you happy is something impossible or impractical to achieve, you are measuring your efforts against a goal that is not achievable. It's a failure before you even start. Goals should be realistic and achievable so they you can experience the exhilaration of working up to your potential. Your goals should be defined so that you are motivated to lean in and do the work required to meet them.

Examining emotions for clues

Our emotions are indicators of unmet needs. Marshall Rosenberg, author of *Nonviolent Communication*, points out we tend to express our needs indirectly through the use of evaluations, interpretations, and images. A person may say to a partner "I feel like you never understand me." This is an indirect expression of a need to be understood. But what the partner most likely hears is a criticism of their disinterest, ineptitude or incompetency. When someone hears anything that sounds like criticism, the normal reaction is to go into the self-defense mode. Defensiveness erects a barricade that shuts down communication and understanding. The more a self-centered co-parent can directly connect feelings with needs and articulate them, the easier it will be to take control over fulfilling those needs, especially when interacting with the other parent.

Unfortunately our culture does not put much emphasis on pinpointing our emotions and expressing them precisely. We rely on words like "angry" and "mad" to cover a long list of more specific emotions. Your first task is to examine the abstract ball of emotional reactions and pare it down the specific emotions you are feeling. You may wish to consult the more extensive list in Rosenberg's book that lists emotions we feel when our needs are met and the emotions we feel when our needs are not met. (*See Appendix 5* – Identify your emotions and needs).

Examine the thoughts you have in connection with specific emotions. What thoughts, positive and negative, do these emotions evoke? Try to be as specific as possible and write down your thoughts. Be careful to identify an actual feeling and not just an opinion that is not actually a feeling. It is common to say "I feel that..." as a description of what we are thinking. That is actually an opinion. Try to identify your specific emotions without saying "I feel that ..." Compare the following:

> "I *feel that* you are irresponsible as a parent."

> "I *feel overwhelmed* with carrying so much of the load."

The first statement is an opinion. It will be received by the co-parent as a criticism. The second statement is the identification of a feeling that the parent is having - being "overwhelmed."

The final step is to take an overview and evaluate your thoughts.

What is not being taken care of?
What do you wish you had more of?
These are the needs you want to satisfy.

"I am *overwhelmed*."
"I am tired and frustrated."
"I need more help."
"I need *more resources*."

Once the needs are identified, then you can set goals for problem-solving. Your need for more help and more resources is the problem you can work to solve.

An example of examining needs

Pat is waiting in the parking lot at a fast food restaurant for the co-parent to arrive with their child for a scheduled exchange. Once again, as so often of late, the co-parent is running late. How thoughtless! The time specified in their parenting plan for the exchange comes and goes. Pat tries to be patient, but as the minutes pass Pat's head starts pounding. Pat chest grows tight and Pat senses the anger rising. As Pat becomes aware of these symptoms Pat stops to think about what the emotional response is signaling. Is "anger" the specific emotion Pat is feeling?

Pat decides to evaluate this further. For one thing, Pat feels disrespected because the co-parent is not taking care to be more punctual. Pat has other things to do beside wait on the convenience of the co-parent. The co-parent's disrespect is also irritating. What needs are not being addressed? Pat is interested in having a predictable time for exchanges. That would be some acknowledgment that Pat's time is valuable too. Reflecting further, Pat also realizes that there is an undercurrent of fear. Has there been an accident? Has the co-parent decided to withhold the child and not make the exchange? What Pat needs is more information and reassurance that exchanges will take place. From this internal conversation, Pat determines to think about ways to increase the predictability of exchanges, reduce delays, and provide for a notification procedure when delays occur.

Thinking outside the box

Informed decision-making is the corner stone of self-centered co-parenting. We all have an innate tendency to go along with the standard options that occur to us, hoping they will meet our needs, instead of exploring what really satisfies our needs and interests. When we lack experience, lack information, or lack adequate feedback, we are likely to rely on assumptions that may not be accurate, or worse, entirely false. This deprives us of the chance to select from more options that reduce and manage the problem. Well-chosen options with preferable outcomes are much more desirable than uninformed default choosing. To think outside the box of unverified assumptions and defaults, it is necessary to suspend judgment, gather accurate data, and reduce the impact of bias in reaching conclusions.

Relying on unverified assumptions can easily lead us astray and keep us from resolving disagreements. For example: Jason wants his son to have the opportunity to play intramural sports. His son brought him a flier about a community football team and seemed excited to participate. The parenting plan provides that each parent will pay one-half of extracurricular activity fees that both parents agree upon. Jason calls the co-parent to make arrangements to enroll their child. The co-parent refuses to contribute.

Jason cannot be really sure why the co-parent refused without further discussion, but he reaches his own conclusion by filling in the gaps with assumptions. Jason's thought process goes like this: *"The co-parent is opposing this because it was my idea. The co-parent is selfish to deprive the child of this opportunity."* Jason's thoughts have undermined his motivation to seek a better outcome. Jason can give up at this point, telling the child he cannot participate and blaming it on the co-parent. Jason can choose to enroll his son anyway and bear the entire cost of the activity himself. He still has the problem of gaining the cooperation of the co-parent to get their child to practices and games. Jason can choose to pursue getting the co-parent to pay half the fees in Court. The time, effort, and money involved make this choice more costly, plus Jason still may not have a commitment from the co-parent for getting their child to practices and games. What gets completely overlooked is the opportunity to reach a better outcome by examining the true motivations and reason behind the co-parent's refusal. By addressing some of the other parent's concerns, the "no" might become a "yes."

We can expand our options by putting more reliance on verifiable facts and refraining from unconfirmed conclusions. The role of assumptions in decision-making was described by Chris Argyris as the *ladder of inference*. We start at the base of the "ladder" with an observation or an experience. We climb the first rung of the ladder by selecting data from the observation or experience that we find important or relevant. Climbing another rung, we affix a meaning to the data we have selected and make our assumption. Next we use our assumptions to fill in the gaps in our understanding in order to give the data meaning that fits within our personal frame of reference. At the top rung of the ladder we use these assumptions to draw conclusions that become fixed as "beliefs" and serve as the basis for our actions. When our beliefs and actions are not grounded in accurate assessment of a situation we are swaying at the top of the ladder of inference, at risk of being toppled. A self-centered co-parent is grounded by taking action based on verifiable data.

When we make decisions leaning only on our assumptions, we leave a lot of information on the table that can be useful in helping us pursue a better choice that meets our needs. Think of problem-solving as a maze. Some pathways will lead to dead ends, but other paths will lead to solutions. Basing decision solely on unverified facts and assumptions cuts us off from valuable paths that may lead to a satisfying resolution of the problem. Assuming we "know" the motivation of the other parent is often based on our negative reactivity, not verifiable information. An unexplored pathway should not be the cause of missing the best way out of the maze.

Comparison of facts and assumptions

Facts are information, events, acts, or circumstances that are observable, verifiable, and based in reality (objective). Decisions based in fact address the actual needs and issues, and avoid tripping into an endless maze of misdirection.

Assumptions are theories based on self-selected data (subject to bias). Assumptions are implied, inferred, based on unconfirmed opinion or rumor. Instead of verifying data, we rely on our own experience and understanding. Decisions are based on what's in our head instead of reality.

A better decision is reached by reducing the impact of bias inherent in our assumptions and increasing the reliance on objectivity based on facts. Jason took rejection of his idea as a dead end. He then substituted his own assumptions as an explanation of the problem and made a choice to do nothing, which was less satisfying for himself and his child. Jason may have guilt feelings about being inept to address the issue for his child. A better tool within Jason's control is the informed decision-making process, which is discussed more fully in Chapter Three.

Jason made his own assumption about the reason the co-parent didn't agree to the intramural activity. That is not the same as *knowing* the reason. Commit to dealing with verifiable information instead of unverified assumptions.

● What do you take for granted without further examination?
(*Jason: the co-parent always rejects my ideas*)

● What thoughts are rooted in beliefs instead of facts?
(*Jason: the co-parent is selfish*)?

● Gather as much data as possible before drawing conclusions.
(*Jason: my son is interested in intramural football, each parent is*

ordered to pay half of activity fees we agree on, the co-parent does not agree. I do not know why the co-parent doesn't agree.)

The actual reason the co-parent was opposed to the intramural activity could be: concern about the activity interfering with other activities; concern that the child's schedule was being overloaded with too many activities, concern about the injury risks of football, concern about the time and cost involved with transportation for the activity. You may be able to think of additional reasons for concern.

The decision-making process is improved when we have a verifiable understanding of the co-parent's concerns. This is discovered through the process of asking the co-parent for more information. In this manner Jason has greatly expanded his options for satisfying his interest in enrolling his child in intramural football.

• When cost is the concern, Jason has the option to agree to pay a larger share of the fees (usually cheaper than court and resolved in a more timely manner).

• When transportation to practice and games is the concern, Jason has the option to work out arrangements to provide transportation when needed.

• When the activity itself is the concern, Jason and the co-parent can discuss managing the risk of injury and/or explore other sports activities for the son's participation.

▶ When the co-parent's concern is loss of parenting time, Jason has the option to offer to adjust parenting time so their child can participate and they both feel the arrangement is fair.

There is an important reason why you should care about what the co-parent thinks. Agreement only occurs when it includes some terms that each parent can agree to. People are willing to agree, even with reservations, when:

1) it meets the best interest of their child, and/or
2) it meets their own needs, and/or
3) their concerns are adequately addressed or diminished.

When the important factors are addressed the likelihood of reaching an agreement and gaining the co-parent's commitment to the decision is significantly increased. Commitment is a foundation block of duration agreements. Commitment is something achieved by mutual decision-making. There is no guarantee of commitment to performing something that is forced, such as a demand or threat.

Even when the co-parent won't agree or commit, by addressing these factors in your self-decentered decision-making process, you increase the likelihood that the co-parent's resistance is reduced. Resist the temptation to become preoccupied with the unfairness of no cooperation and focus on what is within your control.

Here are some common problems and self-centered methods you might use for gaining control to meet your needs and the needs of your child:

● **The co-parent won't give me contact information.**

This can be a serious safety and security issue depending on the circumstances. If you have an accident or healthcare emergency, who can you call to take care of the child? If the co-parent had an accident or healthcare emergency, how will you find out where your child is and who is providing care? Assess how serious a threat this really is. Perhaps you can design a backup plan reaching out to the co-parent's friends and family in an emergency. If your child is old enough to know and remember contact information, teach your child how to get in touch with you (but avoid putting your child in the middle by asking her to spy or tattle on the co-parent). If the child is sufficiently responsible to manage it, arrange for your child to have a cheap phone with limited minutes that can be used in an emergency. You can also try to persuade the co-parent there are other good reasons to provide contact information: it may be required by an insurance carrier, healthcare provider, school authorities; or it may be needed to complete tax returns.

Evaluate why the co-parent is withholding the information. Has contact information been used in the past for repetitious, harassing, or belligerent phone calls? Has the address made it possible to instigate police calls or child protection wellness checks? Confrontations make it less likely the co-parent wants to share contact information. Plan to make your problem-solving efforts more positive and constructive in the future. You may also consider hiring the services of a Parenting Coordinator who can maintain contact with both of you and serve as the go-between in emergencies.

If you have completely lost contact with the co-parent and your child, resolve not to allow this to continue. The longer you are out of contact, the harder it will be to reconnect with your child. Seek information about the co-parent's location through social media and online locator services. See if you can get information through the postal service, the driver's license registration office, or the school your child last attended. Consider hiring a private investigator. A lawyer may be able to help you find the parent through the federal Parent Locator Service.

- **The co-parent won't share information about our child's healthcare.**

This seems particularly outrageous because your child's health is so fundamental to your child's well-being. It the healthcare concern is really serious, such as not sharing information about asthmatic attacks or inhalers, you may want to consider obtaining a court order that sets out a specific procedure for direct access to healthcare information, medications, and equipment. When the issue is maddening but not life-threatening, consider what is within your own control. In some states each parent has a right to healthcare information unless restricted by a court order. In others it may not be specifically provided for by law. Healthcare providers tend to be more accommodating if you have a legal right to the information. The healthcare provider may be willing to accommodate your requests, particularly if you provide the healthcare insurance for the child. You must approach staff with a friendly request, not a demand. Be reasonable and grateful in accepting whatever accommodations they can provide. Remember they have restrictions on what they can provide given patient confidentiality and federal HIPPA regulations. Do not antagonize them or put the provider in the middle of a disclosure dispute between you and the co-parent. Maybe you don't even know the identity of the healthcare providers. If you carry the healthcare insurance for the child, your insurance company will have information about the healthcare providers based on claims that have been made.

Be careful about pumping your child for information. You don't want your child in the middle of this dispute either. Depending on the age of the child, they may or may not know the information. Take a cue from your child's comments about the seriousness of the healthcare concern. You can obtain your own supply of over the counter medications for the child's use during your parenting time. Check into getting a duplicate prescription for medications (this may affect what insurance will cover). If the only way to obtain necessary information seems to require the cooperation of the co-parent, answer these questions: 1) is this necessary to meet the best interest of our child, 2) what is required to address the concern the co-parent has about sharing this information, 3) what can I do to reduce the co-parent's concerns about sharing healthcare information about our child?

• **The co-parent interferes with phone calls I make to the child.**

Answering the phone or accessing the internet for video chats in one's own home is a privacy issue where the courts have limit authority. A judge can order a parent to provide access to the phone or not to monitor calls, but as a practical matter they cannot make a person do so in real time. The legal remedies will only come into play after the infringement. Understand that you cannot control or force the co-parent to engage in phone calls in most cases. (An order for supervised calls may be worth considering, but it will have costs associated with it). Do not expect cooperation with phone calls if this is not the way you currently conduct most of your co-parenting business.

The co-parent may be denying phone access because they are still going through the emotional separation process and are not yet ready to re-engage in a business-like manner. As you move to a less intimate relationship this is likely to change, but will take time and your patience. In other cases, avoidance of phone use is a response to unpleasant previous interactions. Avoid repetitive calls, especially during the child's time with the co-parent. Do not alarm the child during calls by discussing parenting disputes or reminding the child how much you miss them or worry about them. This makes the child feel guilty, but he does not have the power to fix your feelings. Phone access is only under your control in your own home. It may be wiser to put your attention into strengthening your bond with your child during your own parenting time.

● **The co-parent does not return the child's clothing and belongings at the end of parenting time.**

This is another common bone of contention between parents. Providing clothing and equipment that is not returned can be costly as well as frustrating. When a parent cannot afford to replace it or replace it with similar quality goods, the child suffers. For younger children, it may be appropriate not to send valuable belongings to the other parent's house if there is no predictability to returning them. This may just be a matter of lack of diligence by the co-parent, rather than an intention to prevent return of the child's belonging. Mention to the co-parent how much you appreciate their attention to returning items, and ask them to let you know what you can do to facilitate return of items on your end. Teach your child how to become responsible for managing her own belongings. Preteens and teens often express the desire to have control over their own stuff. That privilege comes with the responsibility to manage their stuff. When the child is old enough to be accountable for belongings, it is the child's job to retrieve belongings left with the co-parent. Do not infringe on the relationship between the child and co-parent. Let them try to work it out themselves. After several calls, the co-parent may become more vigilant about the return of belongings to avoid the hassle of multiple trips.

Put what your child needs above any desire to send the other parent a message. Some parents choose to send the child with the same clothing over and over. This can be demeaning for your child, so keep that in mind. Be sure that what you send fits well and is for the activities that will take place during the other parent's parenting time. Do not refuse to send a coat in bad weather, which seems petty.

Children are known to engage in a form of manipulations by whining about clothing, toys, and games that are only available at the other parent's home. Do not buy into that guilt trip. You do not want to engage in a bidding war with the co-parent for your child's approval. It is not necessary to duplicate in your home what the other parent provides. Your positive relationship with the child is priceless compared with a relationship based on physical possessions.

- **The co-parent won't honor my right of first refusal to provide childcare when it is needed.**

This is another slight that can enrage a parent. In most cases, a child's interests are served by care provided by a parent over a commercial day care or unrelated person. A "first refusal" clause contained in a court ordered parenting plan can be enforced by contempt. The proof required to show that those opportunities arose and that the co-parent intentionally failed to notify you of the right of first refusal can be a problem. If you suspect this is happening it is advisable to check with your lawyer about ways to documents the infractions. More explicit procedures in a court order for making right of first refusal calls may be advisable.

What is in your control is to build bridges that make it less troublesome to give notice of your opportunities to provide childcare than to ignore you as a resource. Figure out who are the alternate caregivers. If it's family or friends, let them know in a friendly way that you are willing to serve as backup. It will further influence them positively if you are willing to go the extra mile when you are called on, such as responding quickly or providing transportation both ways. You become a helpful resource instead of a hassle.

When a commercial childcare provider is being paid for providing care when you are available, point this out to the parent as a potential cost savings. Sometimes a provider is going to charge a weekly or monthly fee to hold a place for the child, whether care is provided or not. Check into the childcare provider policies and try to figure out ways that using you is a plus for the co-parent who must make the call to honor your right of first refusal. Try not to antagonize the co-parent when establishing a call procedure. Make it as easy as possible for the co-parent. You want the co-parent to view you as a first resource, not a right of first refusal obstacle.

● **The co-parent is causing problems at our child's school.**

School is the place where your child needs to concentrate on learning not disruptions caused by parents. Pledge to make school a neutral site for your child. School can actually serve as a helpful buffer for exchanges. Instead of being annoyed that the co-parent wants to do exchanges of the child at school rather than at your home, see this as a neutral exchange site and means of peaceful transfer at a time your child is naturally in transition.

Check the school policies to determine when parent visit are encouraged and discouraged. Try to abide by the policies and don't escalate the dispute with school staff. Maintain a calm and reasonable demeanor even if you think you are in the right. At school it's about your child, not your principles. Pick the right time and place to address concerns. Making a scene only embarrasses you and your child. If the disruption crosses the line, school authorities will take action to remove or bar a disruptive parent from school grounds.

Should your name not be listed as a parent contact in the school records, provide the school staff with a copy of any court order that grants you the right of access to school information. Provide your contact information and even self-addressed and stamped envelopes, if necessary, to facilitate the school's contact with you. Develop a relationship with your child's teacher and school principal, so they see you as an ally in educating your child.

Both parents will be allowed to come to school unless there is a court order or their behavior is disruptive. To preserve the peace you may want to arrange separate times for teacher conferences or visits during school time. At activities, like soccer games and choral concerts that both parents may attend, be respectful but keep your distance from the co-parent. Allow your child to interact with the co-parent in his own way. Do not hover over the child and prohibit the child from acknowledging the presence of the co-parent. It is self-affirming for the child to appreciate that both parents care enough to attend these functions.

● **The co-parent won't take our child to softball practice.**

You should anticipate disappointment if you sign your child up for activities that occur during parenting time without first consulting and obtaining the consent of the co-parent. Unilaterally enrolling your child is an activity that takes place over both parent's parenting time without consent oversteps respectful boundaries and will be seen as an invasion of the other parent's time. Boundary violations are quick to ignite an emotional reaction that is likely to overcome consideration of the child's interest in the activity.

You may have to live with the lack of cooperation for the duration of this activity if you didn't obtain the co-parent's consent. Speak with the coach about the situation. You may be able to get some understanding to bend the rules about practice attendance, or an agreement to substitute a clinic or some other activity during your parenting time as an alternative. If the coach holds firm on the attendance policy, have the coach explain this to your child. Some things in life just don't work out and your child needs to learn to deal with disappointment in a constructive way. Do not pull your child from the activity and blame the co-parent for it. This is a self-inflicted wound for which you have responsibility. Pledge to obtain the co-parent's cooperation for future activities, or only enroll your child in activities that allow you to schedule attendance on your own parenting time.

When the co-parent has enrolled the child in an activity that also occurs during your parenting time you have a choice about whether to cooperate or not. Resist the temptation to oppose it just to signal your disapproval of the disrespect shown to you by the other parent's unilateral decision. Think seriously about whether this is a good activity for the child, and one that has captured the child's interest. If you decide to honor the child's commitment to an activity, you should do so without complaint. A self-centered co-parent is a problem-solver, not a victim. If you decide this is worth addressing with the co-parent, do so in an educational and non-defensive way. Do it in writing so you can review and polish what you want to say instead of blurting out your frustration during an exchange or phone call. Here is an example of an educational and non-defensive statement:

> *"I intend to take our child to softball practice during my parenting time this season since our*

child is interested in doing so. In the future I ask for advance notice before you decide to sign our child up for an activity that takes place during my parenting time. I want to have the opportunity to let you know whether I can accommodate the time and transportation involved. Please seek my consent in advance in the future to be sure you have my cooperation."

If the co-parent's unilateral decision-making about activity enrollment continues, consult the section on manipulation in Chapter Three.

• The co-parent won't enforce my decision to ground our child from television.

This is another self-inflicted frustration if you and the co-parent have not previously agreed on a joint discipline policy that you will both enforce in both homes. The only way a unilateral decision to impose a discipline penalty will work is if the co-parent trusts your judgment implicitly and is willing to enforce your decision without question. This is highly unlikely when you have not reached a specific mutual agreement on discipline. If you had reached such an agreement, an educational and non-defensive statement to the co-parent may fix this. For example:

"Our child was restricted from television last week because he was disrespectful about doing his homework for three days in a row. We decided previously that doing homework was very important. I will try to notify you in advance when discipline is imposed in my home in the future. If you have questions or disagree with the decision to restrict television in the future, please know you are welcome to discuss it with me."

When there is no agreement to coordinate discipline your attention is better directed toward applying discipline solely in your own home as part of your own relationship with your child. You have no control over what the co-parent does in the co-parent's home. You must focus on the behavior you expect in your home, and troubling as it seems, leave what happens in the co-parent's home up to the co-parent. Do not let the child manipulate both parents by making the discipline the focus of a dispute. If the co-parent confronts you, at your child's urging, about your discipline decision, you must decide where to set your boundaries. Using one parent against the other is the child's way of manipulating you to bend the disciplinary rules.

Discipline methods need to adjust as your child gets older. As your child reaches school age, discipline becomes a matter of education instead of rule-making. As your child reaches puberty, discipline becomes a matter of reinforcing positive behavior. There are many good books on positive discipline. Despite what happens in the co-parent's relationship, by setting acceptable standards for your child in your home, your child is learning positive behavior that is valuable as your child becomes a young adult. Eventually, your child will make his own decisions about how to conduct himself. Make the best impression possible by focusing on your own relationship instead of trying to control the decision-making in the other parent's home.

Focus on what is in your own control

Many of the things that bug you about the co-parent's behavior can be self-regulated. Concentrate on what is in your control: managing your own feelings, thinking about the impact on your child, and problem-solving to address issues as best you can. When it is necessary to gain more cooperation of the co-parent, forcing has limited value. Positive influence you can exert is much more effective.

CHAPTER 3
Self-Centered Decision-making

Moving from victim to problem-solver

A crucial step in becoming a self-centered co-parent is to change your mindset from victim to problem-solver. It is certainly easy to fall into the role of victim. Things have happened which were unexpected, we did not want, and probably did not deserve. In a victim role we feel powerless. We seek vindication through blame and revenge. We look for a champion who can make things right for us. Even if we attain our goal of vindication, there is no guarantee that it satisfies our actual needs and concerns. Victimhood is centered in the emotional part of our brain. A self-centered co-parent takes note of how consequences are a part of the interactions with the other parent. A self-centered co-parent must rely on problem-solving skills to reach satisfaction of their own needs and the best interest of their child. Submitting to the emotions of victimhood is not empowering. Problem-solving is based in rational thought that manages emotions. A self-centered co-parent understands the interplay of the emotional and rational parts of the brain and how they influence our thoughts. (*See Appendix 1:* How our emotions sabotage problem-solving).

A self-centered co-parent takes control by positively influencing the other parent's behavior and decision-making in ways that serve the best interest of the child. Believe it: the other parent is susceptible to your influence (just as you are influenced by what the other parent does). Influence is a precious commodity. You don't want to squander it by making poor decisions about the most effective way to exert your influence. It cannot be emphasized enough that prudent choices must be made. Forcing and punishing strategies commonly relied on in a victimhood mindset have inherent problems that will undermine the other parent's motivation to cooperate.

In a problem-solving mindset, a self-centered co-parent asks a different set of questions than are asked in a victim mindset. These questions are empowering:

> What am I learning?
> What is useful about this?
> What do I need?
> How can I achieve my goal?

The problem-solving mindset

For example, Dana is frustrated that the co-parent does not share information about their child's educational progress and school activities. In a victim mindset, Dana's thoughts might be: this isn't fair; I am entitled to respect as the co-parent; I have a right to the information; the co-parent is winning and I am losing; how can I make the other parent stop this? The goal is focused on defeating the co-parent. This does practically nothing to achieve the underlying concerns about the child's education. That concern is displaced by a fixation on the competition.

In a problem-solving mindset, Dana's questions are different:

• What am I learning? *I can't depend on the co-parent to feed me information.*

• What is useful about this? *It has brought to my attention that this information is important to me in order to help my child.*

• What do I need? *I need to have access to this information about my child and my child's school activities.*

• What is my goal? *I will find a way to get this information without relying on the co-parent.*

• How can I achieve my goal? *I will contact the school and explore how to get this information directly. If necessary I will ask the court to grant me access to this information.*

The problem-solving mindset is pro-active and empowering. It focuses on Dana's concerns for the welfare of the child and things that Dana has some control to achieve.

Short term and long term decision-making

When making decisions it is necessary to be keenly aware of the impact of your decision in the short term and long term. There will be decisions that require a *quantitative* decision, such as the affordability of an activity fee, and others that require a *procedural* decision, such when activity fee payments will be made and how the parents will split the cost.

Quantitative decisions can easily become a struggle over how much one gets or gives. Emotions become quickly engaged, with all the attendant baggage that accompanies it. The decision may be difficult and stressful to make, but once made it is over except for the implementation.

Implementation is a process that can involve many decisions. For example, the decision on residential custody for your child's parenting plan may be contentious. Once made, however, this is the base line for moving forward. There will be many future procedural decisions to be made: making exchanges of the child for time with the co-parent; coordination of the child's activities that overlap both parents' parenting time; changes to the parenting time schedule to accommodate work, vacation, and other special events.

Recurrent decisions need to take into account the long term consequences and goals of co-parenting. It is possible to make decisions that favor what you prefer in the moment without worrying about the fall-out. Your child is better off, however if you also consider whether the decision increases the stress between parents that diminishes the quality of your child's environment. Is your decision pushing the co-parent to become more competitive with you or is it encouraging the co-parent to be more cooperative? Procedural decisions have consequences for the future working relationship between you and the co-parent. Think about the long term effects.

The limits of forcing cooperation

You have probably given significant thought to what the co-parent should or shouldn't do. A wise maxim says if wishes were horses everyone would ride. Your ideas about what the other parent should or shouldn't do will not be embraced by the other parent unless the other parent decides it is a good idea. There is no requirement for the co-parent to do you any favors. Co-parenting is now a business proposition, not an emotional relationship. Getting things done in the best interest of your child without unnecessary depletion of time, energy or resources is equivalent to being profitable in business. Time-consuming, energy-draining, and resource-devouring tactics are business expenses. When these costs exceed the benefits your business cannot be profitable. That is the definition of business failure.

Put your energy into things within your control. By now you are starting to see that even in the best case scenario it is costly and difficult to "make" the co-parent do or stop doing things. On the other hand, if the co-parent views the decision you also prefer as in their own self-interest, and hopefully in the best interest of your child, they will adopt it without demands or forcing.

Here are a few of the things that are not in your control:

- making the co-parent adopt the same goals you have
- making the co-parent adopt your child-rearing practices
- making the co-parent adopt your priorities

What is in your control, however, is deciding what you are going to do when you don't get the cooperation that will allow you to meet your needs or address your concerns for effective parenting for your child. Your strategy is to craft procedures that influence the co-parent to cooperate, or at least, not disrupt effective parenting on your part.

When the co-parent offends you

A self-centered co-parent takes responsibility for managing emotions and measures responses and actions even when the words and action of the co-parent are offensive. Remind yourself that you have switched your frame of reference from the partner relationship to the parenting relationship. This is about parenting business now *not* emotional attachment. Notice what buttons are being pushed. Dedicate your energy to parenting in the present, not nursing grievances that are holdovers from the past. You want your response to be appropriate and proportionate so that it furthers positive parenting interactions. Think about being assertive instead of just aggressive.

Recognize how your should and shouldn't expectations of the other parent disempower you. You can't influence the co-parent's behavior in a good way by pointing out their faults. The co-parent will resist imposition of ideas under duress or by force. Even if you are able to dominate or manipulate, circumstances that allow you to force your will on the other parent only align temporarily. The costs in time, energy, and resources to continue to exert control over the co-parent is diverting your time, energy and resources from parenting your child. When you no longer have the power to dominate, the co-parent's resentment over loss of freedom of choice will pay you back with more resistance and even less cooperation. Even worse, the co-parent may gain the upper hand and force you to do things you don't want to do. Focus on the needs, concerns, or principles at stake for you and focus on productive ways to take care of parenting business for your child.

It's crucial to pick your battles wisely and engage the co-parent productively. Is the offense worth the time and energy to address it? Can it be resolve directly? What else can you do that is more productive and satisfying? You may find that the offense is a challenge to develop your skills instead of relying on an unproductive response. If you decide it's not worth the fight, appreciate what you have learned by examining these questions and what it is teaching you.

Beware: over-use of power mechanisms

Power plays have the temporary capacity to influence or direct the behavior of others or the course of events. Power is hard to maintain indefinitely. Power plays also have significant side-effects you may want to avoid.

+ **External authority**. This power mechanism relies on the power of a third party to insist on performance or compliance. Since court proceedings are frequently involved in the resolution of parenting disputes, a common authority mechanism is to appeal to the judge to lay down the law (hopefully to the other parent). Parents usually ask a judge to find the other parent in contempt in hopes that that is going to "fix it." Later they are frustrated when it did not have the impact on the co-parent that they anticipated.

Parents often remark that a judge's ruling didn't go as far as they would like. More "punishment" seemed justified. Bear in mind that in a family law case, the judge's main focus is to determine what is in the best interest of the child. Judges are reluctant to impose punishment that negatively impacts the child. Judges find it prudent to keep the consequence in proportion to the problem. For example, a judge won't terminate parental access because the child does not have a bed of his own at the co-parent's house. Less severe remedies will be considered first, such as approving suitable alternatives (cot or sleeping bag) or temporarily suspending overnights until suitable equipment is provided.

Exerting authority is also dependent on a judge finding you are in the right. There is the possibility that a judge may rule in favor of the other parent. Another possibility is that a judge may not agree on the extent of the violation. Reasonable excuses for not following a court order will usually be considered, especially if it promotes the best interest of the child. For example, a parent's failure to turn the child over to the other parent at an exchange of parenting time is not a slam-dunk if the parent picking up the child does not possess a valid driver's license, age appropriate child restraint equipment, or appeared to be too impaired to drive at the time.

Reliance on third-party authorities can be time-consuming. Very few matters are decided in family court unless both parents have advance notice and an opportunity to appear and have their say first. The multiple procedural steps take time. In the meantime the family is living in real time. Months may pass by. Time and opportunities are lost. Certainly, there are occasions in which only an external authority is the appropriate remedy. Expand your repertoire of other strategies for gaining control that are less time consuming, less stress-inducing, and just as effective.

• **Lopsided resources**. One parent may have more resources at their disposal than the other parent. Resources may include money, knowledge, business or social connections, etc. Power can be based in legal rights, the best interest of the child, even public opinion. When a parent decides to use their resources against a co-parent with fewer resources to squelch freedom of choice, the power play absolutely creates resentment and a desire to retaliate when possible. Circumstances tend to shift over time and the source of power changes as a result. Payback for abuse of power is not only unpleasant; it perpetuates conflict that does not have a child-centered focus.

• **Domination**. One parent may insist on calling the shots based on the force of their personality or assertiveness. The other parent may accommodate this when the issue isn't worth fighting over. Sometimes the accommodating parent does so in an effort to reduce conflict or relive stress on the child. When the role of one parent is diminished, the contribution of that parent is also diminished. A parent who feels they have no voice or stake in the life of their child is more likely to detach and not stay involved with their child. While this may seem a desirable result for the dominating parent, the child's inherent right to draw on the resources of both parents has been undermined. The opposite of dominance is leadership. A self-centered co-parent sets the tone for decision-making by exerting influence through leadership to encourage the co-parent to make a positive contribution.

• **Manipulation**. Manipulation is a power grab based on exploiting a parent's fears of loss that can have a significant negative impact. Manipulation deprives parents of the opportunity to explore multiple ways to achieve what is in the child's best interest. One parent decides what they want and goes for it. It's possible this is the best choice, but without the opportunity to have input you won't know if it is or not. Manipulation is usually presented as an either/or choice. Take-it-or-leave-it propositions come across as disrespectful. Resentment is the chief by-product of manipulation and will generate an emotional reaction that perpetuates dysfunctional co-parenting.
Manipulation is unfair and deprives your child of the benefit of the best decision-making process based on input of both parents. Child development research indicates that there are different times in childhood when Moms and Dads play very important roles in creating the child's sense of security, sense of self, and cultivating positive life skills. Because a parent's impact varies at different stages of childhood, restriction of parental involvement has consequences for the child. A parent who is successful at manipulation, will repeat it over and over. It is best to curtail manipulation.

Parents who feel manipulated can empathize with Jack's situation. Jack had been "going along to get along" for the past two years to avoid nasty confrontations with Jill, his son's co-parent. Jill entered a new relationship last year, and became even less cooperative. Now Jill is demanding a large increase in the amount of child support. Jack is terrified that he won't be able to make it if child support is set at that amount. Jill told him that if he doesn't agree Jill plans to terminate his rights and have her new partner adopted the child. Jack feels he has no choice but to give in to her demand, otherwise he won't have a place in the life of his child in the future.

There are several basic questions to ask about manipulative behavior. Usually the manipulation is posed as a either/or proposition with two unattractive options. The manipulative parent anticipates a decision they want by making the other option more revolting. By arousing fear and creating the emotional reaction manipulation seeks the response: I have no choice. The actual choices, however, may not be as limited as the manipulating parent wants the manipulated parent to believe they are. When you are emotionally charged you are less likely to examine your options realistically. When you sense manipulation, take time to manage your emotions and critically examine the options. Here are some questions to ask about a manipulative proposal:

▶ *Are these really my only options?*
Manipulators often use a false dichotomy - the assumption that there are only two possible solutions. A good negotiator knows there are many points between yes and no. The options presented are exaggerated by design to make it appear there are no other options. Do some investigation to find out if other more acceptable options exist.

▶ *Is the cost of not complying really as portrayed?*
Does the manipulative parent have the resources and power to pull off their threat? The law may not be on their side. It may be too expensive to proceed. There may be other roadblocks or barriers to

doing what they say they are going to do if you don't agree. Do your own investigation to assess the risk.

▶ *Is the proposal within my standards of what is fair?*
There is a knee-jerk negative reaction to manipulation. For the sake of your child, however, it is important to examine whether there is something about the proposal that has merit. To what extent is the request fair and beneficial to your child? Do not reject and end the discussion if a fair counter-offer can be made.

Additional information helps Jack: how difficult is termination of parental rights; what is the likely range of child support; what is the cost and time involved in a contested court proceeding. He can then realistically evaluate the likelihood the co-parent has the resources to follow through and whether this is an empty threat. If the information indicates that some increase in child support is likely, he can decide if it makes sense to make a counter-offer for a smaller increase.

You don't want to be on the receiving end of manipulation, and it is just as dysfunctional to dish it out. When you are making self-centered parenting decisions, it is vital to pledge not to use manipulative behaviors. They may be effective, but the effect is not one that is beneficial to your child.

Boost results with use of a parenting coach

Until you feel you are making headway in gaining cooperation from the other parent, you may benefit from the support and feedback of a parenting coach. A parenting coach has special training in child development, human behavior and negotiation skills that can be a valuable resource as you engage in self-centered decision-making. A parenting coach is an important counterbalance to emotional inclinations and will help you stay on track making choices that are child-centered and satisfy your needs.

CHAPTER 4
Self-Centered Interactions

In the process of centering yourself you will need to re-think the way you interact with the other parent. Stop obsessing about why and how the co-parent should and shouldn't perform. You have no control over when and whether the co-parent will make changes. Interactions with the co-parent are a business proposition moving forward. You want to be successful in getting done what needs to be accomplished. It will have some costs on your part. The trick is to "profit" by your interactions so that the benefits to you and your child outweigh the costs to you to achieve it.

This chapter discussed strategies you can adopt to increase your satisfaction with the level of cooperation you get from the co-parent. Effective ways to engage the co-parent are discussed in the next chapter. These strategies require patience and discipline on your part but they will boost your chances of effective interactions and make your life more predictable in the future.

Think in terms of a business relationship

Redefining your interactions with the co-parent as a business relationship has many benefits. There are clearly defined boundaries; it is less intense; it moves at a slower and more respectful pace; and it focuses on problem-solving rather than trying to resolve simmering emotional conflicts. In business, suppliers, vendors, and customers are people a business owner must work with to derive a profit. If a business owner gets crosswise with them, it diverts attention, energy and money from running the business.

Commit to doing what it takes to conduct your business profitably with the other parent. Here are some of the tasks that help a parent succeed in the business of co-parenting:

▶ **Separate the parent from the problem.** Manage your emotions about the other parent and focus on handling the parenting issue at hand.

▶ **Provide information in a timely and appropriate manner.** This educates the other parent and enhances appreciation of the issues.

▶ **Ask for feedback.** Listening to the other parent does not equal agreeing with the other parent. Acknowledging that the co-parent also has a point of view, even if you don't agree with it, is very valuable for building the two way communication necessary for effective problem-solving.

▶ **Respond to requests from the other parent is a timely and respectful way.** You don't need to be rushed to make a decision, however, letting the other parent know that at least you are aware of the request and considering it will slow down the pace. This also tips off the co-parent that providing more information may help in your decision-making process.

▶ **Be willing to negotiate.** The skills discussed in this book will help you be more effective. If you need support, consider using a parenting coordinator or mediator. They are professionals who have training in how to manage emotions and stay on task.

▶ **Determine what the other parent needs.** There must be something worth agreeing to in order for each parent to consent to a plan. Understand that in order to achieve your goals you will also have to let the other parent satisfy some concerns or priorities. A agreement reached by threat, force or power plays is not durable and stokes the resentment that causes a co-parent to be very less cooperative.

Resentment undercuts cooperation

Resentment is a major factor in the decrease of cooperation. The other parent's resentment may seem very much out of proportion to the circumstances. You can't control the co-parent's resentment. Just be aware that it decreases the motivation to cooperate. Don't be the person who digs that hole any deeper.

Resentment is a combination of disgust, sadness, and the perception of injustice. It is most powerfully felt when there is perception of an injury or betrayal by someone in an intimate relationship. Feelings of resentment may be internalized or expressed openly and aggressively. Resentment can be triggered by an emotionally charged incident or by recollection of past events. It is often related to interactions with a person perceived as having more power or a higher status. Resentment leads the "victim" to cut off communication with the perceived "offender." A self-centered co-parent focuses on parenting the child and avoids emotionally charged words and actions that make resentment worse.

All parents want respect for their role in their child's life. This touches on two of the four basic human needs: belonging and self-esteem. Even if you don't feel the co-parent has stepped up to the responsibilities of parenting, you cannot improve the level of cooperation by diminishing their status. Interact with the co-parent in a business-like manner without continuing to point out authority or power imbalances. Talk *with* instead of talking *at* the other parent. Do not belittle the other parent, but pay them the respect of being your child's co-parent regardless of your personal feelings.

Failure to acknowledge parental strengths and positive acts also causes resentment. Try to find a low key way to acknowledge the positive things the co-parent does. Resentment makes it difficult to restore a feeling of respect between people. Do what you can to honor the co-parent's role for the sake of effective parenting for your child.

The problem of defensiveness

A major obstacle to calm, positive, and productive interactions with the co-parent is defensiveness. When a person hears accusations or atttacks an invisible shield goes up around the listener. No further meaningful communication is received as long as the defensive shield is in place. Defensiveness is a reaction to a perceived threat and kicks in very quickly. When one parent is on the defensive it can lead to reciprocal attacks and a spiral of counter-punches that draws both parents down a bunny trail of unproductive arguing. It can take up to an hour to re-set after an emotional exchange. Until both parents can calm down it is unlikely they will get back on track to discuss the parenting issue at hand.

Be sensitive to defensiveness from both angles. When we are the target, we see the remark or behavior as intentional. When we are the messenger, we tend to see the remark or behavior as not obnoxious or as forgivable under the circumstances. The defensive reaction is perceived differently depending which role we play. When the co-parent gets defensive, it doesn't help to discount the reaction. Use it as a clue to what the co-parent finds bothersome.

Defensive reactions can become deeply rooted behavior patterns. Sharon Strand Ellison, author of *Taking the War Out of Our Words*, explains that defensiveness is self-defeating because it robs us of the ability to see the complexity in the motives of others and causes several self-inflicted wounds. Focusing on self-protection makes us feel less secure. Defending our competence makes us feel less adequate. Reacting defensively shuts down information flow and suspends the education process. Instead, we can use our words as tools instead of weapons.

Awareness of the behaviors that trigger defensiveness will provide you the opportunity to diminish their impact when you see them in your interactions with the other parent.

► **Either/Or Thinking**. This is a mindset that sees only two choice to resolving a problem: one is right and the other is wrong. The possibility of other satisfying solutions isn't even considered. In reality there are very few problems in parenting that only have two ways in which they can be addressed appropriately. When we see resolution only in terms of right or wrong, winning or losing, we become more competitive.

► **Domination.** It is normal to feel threatened when someone else acts like they have the right to tell us what to do. Ultimatums and threats are sure to ignite a defensive reaction. Making decisions that require the other parent's cooperation without the co-parent's input is resented. No one likes to be dominated, excluded, or kept in the dark when they believe they are entitled to information or input into a decision. Behavioral research indicates that people are willing to accept an adverse decision if they have a chance to give their input and perceive the decision-making process was fair. Cooperation is the product derived from joint-decision-making (discussed further in the next chapter). Try to model a negotiating stance based on teamwork. Respect the co-parent as a team member, to the extent they wish to contribute. Recognize the co-parent's needs as part of the team. Identify the co-parent's priorities and try to accommodate those that you can work with. Be sure to tell the co-parent that you are hearing what they are saying without judging the validity of their statements.

► **Self-protection**. Everyone has an ego. We want to feel valued and competent. We will take action to protect our ego by trying to shift blame, make excuses or rationalize our behavior. Separate the person from the behavior. Recognize a defensive reaction for what it is: a reaction, not rational behavior. It doesn't help to confront the reaction. Self-awareness is crucial. In order to deal with defensiveness, our own or in others, it is necessary to be aware that we are having a defensive reaction in order to avoid an emotional hijacking. Knowing your triggers is the advance warning system that will allow your rational brain in step in and manage emotions. It also calms you down so you can seek better insight into the reasons behind the defensive behaviors of others. Explore why the co-parent is feeling threatened. Work to address and reduce the perceived threat.

▶ **Criticism.**   Criticism comes across as blaming, attacking, or discounting competence. Focusing solely on what the co-parent is doing wrong increases defensiveness and decreases motivation to cooperate. Managers know that motivation is based in positive affirmation of strengths and education to strengthen weaknesses. Criticism does not gain cooperation. Replace criticism with neutral statements and questions. Rephrase a criticism into a request for help or a clarification of information. The accusation *"You are always late for exchange of the kids"* can be softened to *"I'm confused about the best time for the exchange. What works for you?"* Reduce aggressive words and tone. Speak slower and in a softer voice. Be respectful, empathize with the concerns the co-parent raises, and respond non-defensively. Sharon Ellison has written a remarkable book about non-defensive communication that will help you build this skill. It is also valuable for interactions with your child. (See Recommended Readings for more information on *Taking the War Out of Our Words.*)

Self-centered editing

A skill that can help you stay on task and in a problem-solving mode with the co-parent is the ability to edit the negative messages that get thrown at you. Taking responsibility for our emotions, rather than blaming others for making us feel a certain way, empowers us to make choices that are best for us and our child. Marshall Rosenberg, author of *Nonviolent Communication*, identifies four ways we can receive a negative message. Options one and two are reactions. Options three and four are pro-active and centering actions that prime us for problem-solving.

Option one: We can take it personally, accept the judgment of others as accurate, and blame ourselves. This may make us feel guilty, ashamed, and undermine our will to proceed.

Option two: We can become defensive and blame the messenger. Our emotional reaction can derail our intention to stay on track.

Option three: We can become aware of our internal feelings and needs and what that is telling us. Rather than allowing our emotions to be dictators, they are valuable as indicators of what we need to carry on. Once we are aware of the reaction and our choices, we can make a strategic decision about how to proceed.

Option four: We can take a look at what is hidden in the message that hints at the feelings and needs of the messenger. That is important information a self-centered co-parent can use to incorporate need-meeting proposals in negotiations.

Living with uncertainty

Not knowing or being able to predict exactly what is going to happen in the future (ambiguity) is stressful. Our imagination is primed by the fears we harbor and we worry about all kinds of bad outcomes. A self-centered co-parent will learn to manage ambiguity so that it does not overpower the ability to make rational decisions. One way to gain some peace of mind is to develop plans for how you will deal with the possibilities. Ask yourself three questions about the unknown you worry about:

1. How realistic is this threat/harm? Am I in harm right now?

2. What resources can I call on to deal with this?

3. What is my plan A, and plan B if plan A doesn't work out?

Having a plan and an alternate plan relieves you of the terror of not knowing what to do in the moment. The more realistically the plan draws on your resources, the more confidence you can have that you are prepared to address a situation should it occur. It is often said that worry is spending 99% of your energy on something that is likely to happen only one percent of the time. Allocate your energy more proportionately to planning for contingencies and the day to day tasks that you really have to manage.

Merging differences in thinking styles

We often overlook the fact that people don't process information and think about it in the same way. Knowing more about thinking styles and the particular thinking preferences that you and the co-parent utilize can help you become a better communicator. (*See Appendix 6* – Role of Thinking Preferences).

Research into the various ways in which people think and interact became popular in the 1960s as corporate managers where attempting to figure out what motivated employees and how to interact with them constructively. An early discovery was that motivation is increased when people need to have their efforts acknowledged and tends to decrease when good work is overlooked by focusing on criticism of less than perfect performance. This is of paramount importance in co-parenting: communications that are only criticisms do not motivate a co-parent to cooperate. Communications should at the least be balanced with recognition of strengths and missions accomplished along with exploration of ways to deal with problems.

A basic understanding of differences in thinking preferences is the tendency of an individual to rely on the "right brain" or "left brain" when engaging in problem-solving. Everyone uses both the right and left side of the brain, but most of us are more comfortable in processing thoughts in one of the two hemispheres of the brain. Left brain people are most comfortable in using language and logic (if A, then B, etc.) Right brain people are more comfortable with imagery, music and creativity – thought may be felt without being expressed. Thoughts are flowing, not linear.

When a left brain dominant person converses with a right brain dominant person adjustments must be made by each to get on the same page. It's not helpful to assume that the other person automatically gets it. A left-brain processor puts stock in words and data. The feelings and ideas that are incorporated into right-brain thinking need words to make them tangible for a left-brain processor. A personal connection so important to a right-brain processor may not even be considered necessary by a left-brain processor. Left-brain processors needs to consider that appropriate social interactions are as important to a right-brain processor as are the words, data, and rules they need for effective communication.

Left Brain Processor	*Right Brain Processor*
ANALYST	VISIONARY
Evaluates using linear thinking (logic). Data driven.	The big picture and how things might be
TASKMASTER	SOCIALITE
Task-oriented. Steps and who performs them.	Connection and positive interaction.

Conversing with someone who does not share the same thinking preferences requires additional effort and input to make sure communication is effective. While a right-brain processor may crave some understanding and enthusiasm about an idea from a left-brain processor, the left-brain processor needs some understanding that time for analysis and procedure development is also important. While a left-brain processor may assume a decision is just about specifying the procedure to accomplish a task, the right-brain processor needs to feel like a respected team member instead of an underling being ordered around. Incompatible needs both require accommodation to avoid the frustration that leads to disconnecting from the conversation.

There are also differences with peoples' thinking styles when they operate out of the same hemisphere of their brain. For example, left-brain processors who are more analytical are easily annoyed with left-brain processors who put a priority on completion of task and compliance with rules. One wants time to evaluate all the upsides and downsides and the other wants to delegate and get on with things.

Thinking preferences can give us some idea on what a parent may focus on in a discussion about selecting a sports activity for their child's participation. The Analyst may focus on the cost and benefit for the child. The Visionary may focus on how this creates future opportunities for the child. The Socialite may be most concerned about how the child will be involved as a team player and treated as an individual. The Taskmaster will assemble information about the practice and game schedule, who will take care of equipment, and how transportation will be handled.

When we are still in an intimate relationship we tend to think this clash in thinking styles is just a lack of caring, disrespect or worse. As the intimacy between co-parents decreases it will become easier to look at the differences dispassionately and develop the patience and willingness required to communicate more fully.

Boost results by using a parenting coordinator

Interactions are likely to be touchy, given the lack of cooperation, until both of you reach the point where it is possible to let go of past hurts and focus on what is best for your child. A parenting coordinator serves as an on-the-spot mediator to interact with both parents in order to support child-centered decision-making. This is a person either appointed by the court, or hired by both parents, to help parents over the rough spots in real time. The parenting coordinator works within the guidelines of your court ordered parenting plan to help parents overcome emotional reactions and engage in decision-making that helps you stay on track making child-centered choices.

CHAPTER 5
Taking the Initiative

Self-Centered Co-Parenting does not make the co-parent irrelevant. There will be times when you need to inform the co-parent about issues involving your child. There will be times when finances or decision-making requires coordination with the co-parent. You may find it crucial at some point to address a problem by seeking the cooperation of the co-parent. As a self-centered co-parent you can do this. The trick is to pick your battles wisely.

You are creating a new way of interacting with the co-parent, and this will take time and effort. When the co-parent is extremely avoidant or extremely combative, even emergency decision-making will be hard until communication channels improve. Your child's safety and security is the best motivation to get busy building your self-centered co-parenting skills.

Why we avoid difficult conversations

Whether to undertake a difficult conversation is a struggle that starts in the recesses of our brain. The amygdala (the emotional center) triggers a fear reaction to emotional memories of past unpleasant conversations. Stress ignites the fight-or-flight response. In the rational center of the brain, on the other hand, we understand that conflict provides an opportunity to influence others and facilitate change. Our brain is assessing all the angles. We have the option of empowering our rational thinking by managing the signals from the amygdala to run. This allows us to face important issues. Preparation for a difficult conversation helps. A self-centered co-parent makes use of mindful and productive strategies. It is self-defeating to allow a fear reaction to dictate your choices.

When to initiate a conversation

Picking your battles wisely involves asking a series of questions and assessing your commitment to having a productive conversation.

1. What is the issue I want to address successfully for my child?

2. Is this issue about something important for the child, separate from my personal emotional motivations?

3. Is this issue important enough to undertake a conversation, or can I live with another option that does not require the cooperation of the co-parent?

4. Will I spend the time and effort it takes to give success a chance?

5. Can I commit to doing what it takes to manage my emotions in order to have this conversation?

When to go to court

At some point it has probably occurred to you that you might avoid the aggravation of dealing with the co-parent by just taking the matter to court. There is a time and place for court, but you should evaluate all your options first. Mark Twain wisely noted that "If the only tool you have is a hammer, soon every problem looks like a nail." Frustrated parents try to shoe-horn their co-parenting relationship problems into the litigation process, but that venue has its limitations when it comes to dealing with interpersonal relations. A thoughtful analysis of the risks and opportunities will help you make a good decision about how to proceed. (*See Appendix 2 – When to go to court*).

Understand the limits of litigation. It further strains the working relationship with the co-parent, but it can bring some structure to the havoc caused by avoidance or constant re-negotiation of choices. When conflict is destructive, interactions are abusive, or decision-making is harmful to the welfare of the child, a court order can establish the ground rules to guide decision-making. The more intense the ongoing conflict, the more specific the ground rules should be. This does take away some degree of freedom of choice and flexibility, so they should only go as far as necessary to add predictability to future conduct. Avoid open-ended terms like "as the parents mutually agree." Too much wiggle room decreases predictability and fails to curb the egocentric decision-making that erodes a cooperative mindset.

Powerful communication tools

You may find it surprising that *listening* is the first topic mentioned in a discussion of powerful communication tools. The fact we have two ears and only one mouth indicates the importance of listening in the process of communication. We cannot absorb information by talking. Listening is our means for receiving information and for getting feedback. Active listening involves removing the personal filters that block out messages with which we don't normally agree. An active listener takes in what is said and is willing to give it consideration (but that does not mean we have to agree with what is said).

Active listening is the way we show our attention and interest to the other person in order to continue a productive conversation. Non-verbal cues provide as much as ninety percent of communicated content. Non-verbal active listening cues include facing the speaker, making eye contact, relaxed physical stance, and smiling or nodding your head (as appropriate). By showing interest, you encourage further conversation that is genuine and respectful.

Active listening is further enhanced by verbally reflecting back what was said to confirm it was heard accurately, even if we don't agree with it. Try to use the words that were heard and don't put any personal spin on it. The speaker's feedback confirms you received the information accurately. You can start a reflection like this "*Am I hearing you accurately, that you are saying ....?*" The speaker will be gratified to acknowledge you heard it accurately or to correct a wrong impression.   Through active listening and feedback you become the recipient of valuable information that can be used in crafting the solution to a problem.

The words we choose can help us make a connection or drive a wedge into a conversation. It can be as simple as substituting the word "we" for the word "you." The focus of the word y*ou* is solely on the other parent as a target for action, criticism, or blame. The word "we"   acknowledges joint parenting responsibility and the benefit of teamwork and cooperation. Using the word "we" as much as possible keeps the focus on gaining cooperation instead of putting the co-parent on the defensive.

Another powerful word that disarms defensiveness is the word "I." When "I" is used to express a concern, disclose a feeling, or share a vision for a better working relationship, it closes a gap. But "I" has the opposite effect when it is used to make a demand, pronounce a decree, or deliver a judgmental point of view. A productive conversation seeks to discover the needs and concerns of the other parent and merge them into jointly acceptable and child-centered solutions. Resist the temptation to pontificate and make demands. Neutralize defensiveness by avoiding accusing, dictating, and preaching.

Consider mediation for difficult conversations

The most difficult conversations we engage in are those in which we have an emotional stake.   The effort to manage our personal emotions while attempting to engage our rational brain can be overwhelming. When the issue is important and we want to make progress, the use of an intermediary can be invaluable. A mediator is a person who has no stake in the problem or dispute other than to help each participant in the conversation feel heard and understood and supported to engage in productive conversation. Mediators have skills that help to shape a discussion around a common goal - your child – that you can both talk about. Mediators use negotiating skills to empower each parent to maximize their possible satisfaction and reduce the downsides in a dispute. Mediation has been integrated into the litigation process in many jurisdictions. Many courts expect parents to engage in mediation before a judge will hear a dispute.

What does a productive conversation look like?

Conversations are valuable as a means of gathering information about the other parent's perspective, hearing the other parent's concerns, and exploring ideas. The foundation for solution to a parenting problem can develop over a series of conversations.

1. The conversation is focused on an issue about the child which is posed in a neutral way, so you are both willing to discuss it.

> Poor: *"I want to talk to you about enforcing the punishment I impose when our child is at your house."*

> Better: *"I'd like to talk about how we might coordinate discipline."*

2. Issues are raised in a non-defensive manner (no accusations, blame, or judging) in order to minimize emotional reactions.

> Poor: *"You never take the initiative to check our child's homework assignments."*

> Better: *"I wonder if our child could benefit from having both of us check homework assignments."*

3. Charged emotions are managed so the conversation can continue. A time out is an acceptable strategy that lets you calm down and have space to think about your options. Honor a time out request by the co-parent for the same reason.

4. Information is exchanged that helps both of you think about possible acceptable solutions instead of fighting over reactive positions that may overlook better options.

5. By the end of the conversation there is a reasonable expectation of action or further conversation about the issue.

Guide for a productive conversation

One of the most important skills you can develop in preparing for a productive conversation is to become aware of your thinking preferences and those of the co-parent. Each one of us harnesses the powers of the left and right sides of our brains to work in tandem. We do not all do it in the same way. Some people are "right brained" - ideas, inspiration and relationships dominate the manner in which we think. Others are "left brained" - language and logic play a more significant role. If your thinking preferences do not mesh with those of the co-parent (and chances are they don't), you can become a more effective communicator by linking thinking preferences with the way in which the co-parent prefers to process information. (*See Appendix 7* – Role of Thinking Preference).

Before you have a conversation, it is necessary to put some effort into preparing for the conversation if you want to increase the likelihood it will be productive.

1. **Decide in advance the child-focused reason for initiating the conversation.** Is the issue one you really want to succeed in addressing? Are you willing to put the time require to prepare for a productive conversation?

2. **Adopt a positive mindset.** Relax. Remain calm and confident. Discard negative predictions of failure and adopt a determination to succeed. Envision this as a team-building exercise to benefit your child. Work on the problem without attacking the co-parent.

3. **Stick to positive statements**. No blaming, judging, or guessing at motives. The words "you" and "but" should be avoided. Be willing to give the co-parent the benefit of the doubt for a while instead of rendering a swift verdict.

4. **Keep the conversation child-centered**. The co-parent is usually willing to talk about your child. It is reasonable for the co-parent to have different ideas (you *both* have a right to disagree). The co-parent still loves your child even when you disagree with each other. You are just expressing your love and concern in different ways. Be willing to hear what the co-parent has to say. You don't have to agree with it but you do have to understand the concerns. Those concerns must be addressed in order to reach agreement. Stay away from judging, blaming the co-parent, or dwelling on the co-parent's shortcomings. Your decision is better when in incorporates each parent's strengths.

5. **Reduce the Heat**. When the topic is sensitive, emotions are easily triggered and can quickly overwhelm the conversation. As emotions heat up, the reactive part of the brain takes over and rational decision-making suffers. To stay on track:

● Don't react to negative expressions of emotion. Try to acknowledge the emotion and stop there. ("*I realize this makes you angry.*") Being heard is a vital first step to engaging in a two-way conversation.

● Following up with a short silence can be a way of giving each of you a brief time out to regain control. Slowing down the pace gives the reactive part of your brain a chance to calm down so you can engage in rational thinking.

● Focus on information, not feelings. Asking boring questions is another way to slow the pace of the conversation until you are both able to focus on the issue (who, what, when, where – avoid why and how).

● Don't feel compelled to defend yourself. This is not a time when it will be heard in a useful way.

6. **Commit to staying on topic**. You put a lot of thought and effort into deciding to initiate the conversation. You decided that this issue was so important for your child that you are taking the risk to address it. Don't let the conversation wander off into uncharted territory. To steer back to the purpose of the conversation when it starts to stray off course, you can say:

"I hear you, but right now we need to discuss … ."

"I'd consider talking about that at another time, but right now let's talk about…."

7. **What are the co-parent's concerns or needs**? Knowing what is really at issue for the co-parent is important. A fix for important needs or concerns must be part of any decision or solution you reach (just as you want the co-parent to address your needs and concerns). Do not guess or assume about the co-parent's needs or concerns. Ask the co-parent to clarify and verify what needs to be addressed from their point of view.

8. **Generate more than two options for solving the problem**. There are many possibilities in addition to "my way" or "your way." Those positions tend to be the polar opposites. Keep an open mind and explore what else could happen. More good choices are possible when you create a pizza buffet that each parent can choose from, rather than forcing consumption from one pizza.

9. **Be patient**. Don't "cut to the chase." Lay the groundwork to establish a respectful two-way conversation first. Be somewhat flexible. This conversation may need to take place in multiple parts. The first discussion may end before you want it to, but you have succeeded in opening the door to future discussion.

10. **Remember this is a process.** Give yourself and the other parent time to process what is said. It may be productive to take a break to gather more information or take time to think about possible solutions. Seek solutions that truly satisfy your needs and promote informed decision-making for your child.

The *magic* of joint decision-making.

Making decisions on your own is fine as long as you are not violating a court order, don't need the cooperation of the co-parent, *and* your decision doesn't tread on your child's right to a relationship with the co-parent. There will be times, however, when you may need the co-parent's cooperation. It's a common mistake to assume that you should decide on the best solution on your own, then present it to the co-parent to agree or disagree.

Unilateral decision-making comes across as demeaning and disrespectful of the co-parent's status. The fear of being shut out by a "done deal" or suspicion that the decision was reached in order to short-change the co-parent is likely to lead to an emotion response, which usually is an emphatic NO! The parent who has taken the time to craft the proposal then views that "no" as very disrespectful of the effort it took to come up with the solution.

Joint- decision-making means involving both parents throughout the process: to identify the problem, suggest ideas, and craft the solution. Avoid the *Either/Or* decision-making orientation. It is adversarial and more emotionally-charged. Competitive bargaining is also more likely to lead to impasse (getting stuck). The chance of resolution when the only choices are yes-or-no is at least 50 percent and usually higher. A basic premise for reaching agreement is this: there must be something in the proposal to which each parent is willing to agree. So besides what works for you, what works for the co-parent is very important. *Both/And"* decision-making incorporates the input and ideas of both parents and seeks to find a solution that maximizes satisfaction for both parents to the fullest extent possible.

Instead of viewing the problem as one "pizza" and the solution as what is your portion of the pizza, think of the problem as requiring a solution based on ideas that can be selected from a pizza buffet. In this way you are expanding your options for agreement instead of competing over one fixed outcome. There are numerous ways your choices come together to reach a compatible resolution. Neither parent may get everything they want, but the goal is for each parent to get sufficient satisfaction out of the solution to agree to some less satisfactory terms as well. (For more about negotiation orientations *See Appendix 8* - Negotiating Styles).

Joint decision-making involves joint effort. It is best to start at the beginning by defining the problem together in a child centered way. After all, your child is what you both have in common. Gather information about interests, needs, goals, and concerns. . There are many ways to parent that are appropriate and effective. By incorporating the variety of needs, concerns, desires and goals, you are using the *Both/And* orientation to create a pizza buffet with sufficient choices for each parent to choose from to reach an agreement. The process of reaching the decision creates buy-in for the solution and builds the commitment of both parents to implementing the agreement.

More on the power of nudges

Agreements, alas, are not always possible. Nudges are a means of having positive influence on the co-parent's decision-making in the absence of agreement. An effective "nudge" is designed to educate the co-parent and present choices in a manner that allows the other parent to compare more and less desirable choices when making a decision whether to cooperate or not. Since a nudge preserves the decider's freedom to choose well or poorly, it reduces the resistance and resentment that usually increases during confrontation or threatening. Most people are able to determine the upsides and downsides of consequences once they are identified. People are prone to make the more attractive and least painful choice. (*See Appendix 6* - Use of Nudges).

The use of nudges is becoming more common for supporting better decision-making in consumer transactions, financial services, and government regulations. At the grocery store you may have seen fresh fruit for sale at some checkout counters instead of customary sugary treats. The ready availability of fruit is a nudge for consumers to choose a healthier choice. It's more effective than a sign directing consumers to return to the produce section to get a healthy snack. A consumer is more inclined to reach for the candy bar instead of getting out of line to make a trip back to the produce section. If the consumer chooses to buy a candy bar at the checkout counter, however, the nudge does not penalize him. The vendor does not have to take ayn action to punish the poor choosing. The consumer pays for his choice by the effect on his own waistline.

This nudge seems like a light touch, but subtle nudges are often the most effective. The vendor could post a sign saying that the sale of candy bars is prohibited. The consumer may view this as a challenge and go out of his way to protest or to go to a different store, as inconvenient as it may be, to buy a candy bar. The consumer may be so affronted that he stops shopping at that store altogether. We are more likely to do things we perceive as our own idea or based in our freedom of choice. We tend to resent being told what we can and can't do.   Freedom to choose lowers opposition and negative reactivity.

A nudge is more effective when it includes information to educate the consumer about consequences and ways to make a healthier choice should the consumer choose to do so. A poster at the checkout counter with dire warnings about the dangers of empty calories is a weak nudge.. The poster has a better impact when it compares the calories in candy bars and fruits and the healthy daily caloric intake. Nudges lay out the choices and consequences and allow the decision-maker to pick the consequence. No one else has to put any time and effort into forcing a choice or penalizing the decision-maker for a poor choice. The consequence is its own reward or punishment.

Nudging the co-parent

Nudges can be used as incentives or disincentives to increase the predictability that the other parent will make choices that also work for you. They can be built into your self-initiated plan, court ordered parenting plan, or agreements with the co-parent. These nudges include consequences to encourage compliance and discourage going off course. They entice the co-parent to choose the preferred option without forcing or threatening. Nudges avoid the use of prohibitions and warnings that increase resistance - the opposite of cooperation.

Think of nudges as ramps onto the superhighway of effective co-parenting. A well-constructed nudge encourages cooperative behavior. Nudges are particularly effective when they *encourage* good parenting. For example, the non-residential parent may have every intention of staying in regular contact with a child. When there is no specific parenting time schedule for contact it is easy for other daily matters to divert that parent's attention. Time passes and performance does not match the intention to stay in touch. A habit of regular contact is not being developed. Infrequent and unpredictable contact affects the child. Over time the child will wonder whether the parent doesn't care and whether she is worthy of the parent's attention. Eventually so much time passes that the parent-child relationship suffers from the neglect. The consequences of irregular contact are separated in time from the day-to-day choices. By the time the parent becomes aware of the consequences the child has suffered considerable emotional turmoil. Vague open-ended plans do not have prompts or scheduled decision points that enhance good-decision-making about contact with the child.

Nudges can be built into a parenting plan which will encourage the parent to take action that establishes a pattern of regular, predictable contact. If these nudges require low or no effort by you to administer, so much the better. Everyone benefits when good decision-making outweighs the cost of the nudge. Here are some low cost contact nudges that can be included in your parenting plan:

▶ Include specifics in a schedule for parenting time in your parenting plan: dates, times, places for exchange, the role of each parent in exchanges. Not only do specifics address the procedures for contacts, they reduce the conflict that may irrupt with constant re-negotiation when the terms are non-specific.

▶ Create reminder prompts for upcoming exchanges. A printed calendar for each parent is an old school method. Technology is available for notification on computers, tablets, cell phones through Google calendar, other invitation apps, or an online parenting subscription service.

▶ Establish a policy to permit adjustment by a predetermined amount of time within a defined period on advanced notice (very useful when work hours fluctuate). This requires even less effort if consent to the adjustment is implied unless otherwise expressed. The method of notification must be specified along with a deadline for replying if the other parent doesn't consent.

▶ Tardiness is a frequent complaint. Set a window for the exchange time. When the exchange happens within that window (say 15 to 30 minutes) a credit accrues, such as additional parenting time tacked on to a holiday or vacation time. Be careful that this calculation isn't burdensome, so keep the formula simple. To avoid future disputes keep a log to track the credits. The log should be accessible to both parents, for example by Google Docs or online parenting service.

▶ Provide for other methods of contact that will be honored when in-person parenting time will not take place as scheduled. The contact can be initiated by the parent or the child, if age appropriate. Access possibilities are: phone, email, or video chat.

► Consider an automatic re-scheduling procedure when scheduled parenting time won't take place due to illness of the child or parent, work conflicts, or other commitments that both parents agree should take precedence (like a family reunion or wedding). Substitute the next following weekend or holiday or some similar period within a reasonable time at the preference of parent who accommodates the change.

► Have a procedure for accommodating transportation for exchanges when a transportation issue arises (i.e. -alternate drivers, splitting cost of public transportation, reimbursement of costs to a parent helping out with transportation).

► Have a policy for how additional child care costs will be handled when a parent does not keep scheduled parenting time.

You will notice that some of these nudges assume you are willing to be flexible. Not all nudges are appropriate for every situation. You should always assess the extent to which there will be consequences for you as well and the extent to which you are willing to tolerate them in order to encourage the co-parent to cooperate.

Here are examples of nudges with a downside (less desirable consequence). They can be effective, but must be used discreetly. Nudges should not create resentment or resistance. You are seeking to give the co-parent the *choice* to cooperate, which builds internal commitment for the co-parent to perform cooperatively.

► A policy to liberally consider requests for change in parenting time submitted by a specific deadline, with an understanding that requests made after the deadline will only be considered in unusual circumstances. For example, consent will granted 72 hours or more in advance in most circumstances; consent within 72 hours only for serious illness or unanticipated work obligations.

▶ Incorporates a short forgiveness period for exchanges with the understanding that if the exchange does not occur within the forgiveness period the parenting time is cancelled, or an amount of equal or greater time is deducted from a holiday or vacation time. A less harsh nudge is to allow a parent to accumulate minutes that can be used as credits when needed for delaying future exchanges on advance notice.

When the co-parent is very uncooperative, however, it is best to reduce them to writing and incorporate nudges into the court-approved parenting plan.   Constantly re-negotiating choices is stressful. Vague terms are subject to frequent re-negotiation, erode a cooperative mindset, and encourage ego-centric decision-making which may not serve the best interest of the child. A specific plan with a degree of flexibility both parents can tolerate is much preferred over an open-ended plan.

Characteristics of effective nudges

Nudges are effective tools for encouraging self-motivated cooperation from the co-parent.   The co-parent is making an independent determination based on what is perceived as in the co-parent's best interest and, to the extent the nudge is crafted appropriately, in the best interest of the child. You create the nudge, the co-parent makes the commitment. Effective nudges have these characteristics:

▶ **The nudge allows freedom of choice.**
Mandates and prohibitions that deprive a person of choice are more likely to create resistance, not cooperation.   Options for choosing should enhance the co-parents ability to make a better choice.   The internal choosing process builds understanding and commitment to implement the choice.

▶ **The nudge includes the best options to maximize satisfaction.**
Choosing is easier when it is apparent that the "best" option fulfills a need or concern and avoids less desirable consequences. Choices we

want the co-parent to pick must be more attractive than the option they might otherwise choose. This means you may need to sweeten the pot by being more accommodating or flexible to the extent that makes sense as a benefit to you or your child.

▶ **The nudge educates the decision-maker about the best choice.**
Make the best choice obvious by including terms or information that support good decision-making.

▶ **It connects current choosing with long-term consequences.**
When reasons to comply over time are not immediately obvious, use a nudge that connects with the long-term consequences of the impending decision. For example, a nudge can encourage a parent to regularly help with the child's homework and thereby avoid the consequences of poor grades when homework is neglected over time.

▶ **The nudge has low administrative costs.**
A self-centered co-parent is seeking freedom from frustration. A nudge should not require a lot of effort on your part. The benefit derived from gaining cooperation should not be outweighed by the burden it places on you. For example, a nudge that reminds the co-parent about the time and date of the next exchange should not take a lot of your time. Automating the nudge is not as burdensome.

Educate with predictions

Prediction is another way of educating the co-parent about the possible consequences involved in choosing. The goal of predicting is to enhance better decision-making by educating the co-parent on your intended course of action depending on the choice made. This establishes boundaries for what you are willing to tolerate and what you are not. You do not engage in an argument or power struggle with the other parent because you are informing the other parent of your choice depending on the choice the co-parent makes.

For example, you can use prediction to encourage the co-parent to make a better decision about whether to take the child to a doctor's appointment. Your goal with the nudge is to help the co-parent understand why the doctor's appointment is important and how the co-parent helps *the child* (not you) by cooperating.

A self-centered co-parent might say:

> "Remember that Junior has to get his sports physical at 10:00 a.m. on Saturday. If you take him to it I will reimburse you for my share of the co-pay when we do our exchange on Sunday night. If you decide not to take him, I will take that as your wish not to schedule the checkups on your time. Unfortunately, you won't be able to get updated on his health care immediately by the doctor."

Predictions must not be framed as threats. Putting the other parent on the defensive is more likely to lead to a negative emotional reaction rather than a thoughtful evaluation. Keep your tone calm and matter-of fact and your demeanor non-threatening. You are simply conveying information. A prediction that set limits can be phrased as an "if ...then" statement informing the other parent how you will respond depending on the choice the other parent makes. A prediction can also be framed to inform the other parent of the likely consequences that will result from their choice. A self-centered co-parent using this prediction technique might say

> "Remember that Junior has to get his sports physical at 10:00 a.m. on Saturday. If you decide not to take him he won't meet the requirements to try out for the team next week."

Predictions should not only inform the co-parent but include a choice about how you will behave that works for you. For example, Judi is frustrated about delays in exchanges on a night when she needs to get to her exercise class. So far the co-parent hasn't taken her requests to arrive on time seriously. Judi can improve the co-parent's decision about being on time for exchanges by making a prediction about her future behavior. She could predict she will leave and call off the exchange altogether. This is heavy handed and doesn't fix her problem. The prediction requires her to either forgo her exercise class or quickly find another caregiver. In addition, the child is deprived of his parenting time with the other parent. If the co-parent doesn't see missed parenting time as a big deal, Judi will be making a lot of trips to the exchange site without obtaining the desired result.

An improved prediction Judi could make is that if the co-parent does not to make the exchange by a certain time, then the child will be taken to the gym and put in the childcare program with the expectation that the co-parent will need to reimburse her for the childcare cost or pay the fee to retrieve the child at the gym. This meets Judi's need to be on time and makes appropriate arrangements for care of the child. She is not overly inconvenienced by following through with this prediction. The child won't be sitting around at the exchange site wondering what will happen next. The co-parent can still have parenting time by going to the gym and paying the childcare fee. But what is the co-parent likely to do? Will the fee motivate the co-parent to be on time or to refuse to come to the gym to pick up the children? Is there a way to hold the co-parent responsible for the cost of child care at the gym without a lot of additional hassle? These are factors Judi must think through in crafting her prediction. A possibility for improving her prediction would be to resolve to drop the child off at the co-parent's mother's house. There won't be any child care costs involved and the care-giver is someone likely to be acceptable to the co-parent and the child. Judi will have to consider if the time and travel involved is practical and whether the grandmother will agree to do this. If grandmother's house is a further distance for the co-parent to travel, the inconvenience might be another motivator to arrive for exchanges on time.

The idea behind an educational prediction is for the co-parent to weight the consequences of the various options available in order to freely decide on the choice that also works best for you. Bear these considerations in mind:

▶ **The consequences must be fully expressed and complete.** To serve as a reliable prediction there should be no need to add or take away from it later. The consequences should be clear.

▶ **Your prediction must be non-negotiable.** This is a tool you are using to let the other parent know you will no longer put up with lack of cooperation. The prediction must solve your problem if the co-parent chooses not to cooperate.

▶ **Consider the possible ramifications of your prediction.** Keep the consequences as small as possible. Try to avoid any foreseeable outcomes that will cause more problems. If you can't live with it, look for a different consequence.

▶ **The consequence should be as limited in duration as possible.** Your prediction should not be perceived as punishment, which fuels Resentment and rebellion and even less cooperation.

▶ **Give the decision-maker control over the duration of the consequence.** This provides free choice while still protecting your boundaries. In our example, if the co-parent misses the exchange time and Judi takes the child to grandmother's house, the co-parent can still have parenting time by going to grandmother's to pick up the child.

▶ **Commit to following through.** For predictions to be taken seriously, you can't negotiate implementation of the consequence. The prediction strategy requires follow through. If the other parent begs for a do-over or apologizes, you will be tempted to give in (violate your boundaries). That strips away the predictability of consequences and boundary protection for you. By following through, the co-parent soon appreciates you are serious.

Boost results with use of a mediator

Until you feel you have resolved and disconnected from an intimate relationship with the co-parent, you will probably find it more comfortable and empowering to negotiate through a mediator. A proficient mediator has non-defensive communication skills and effective negotiation strategies that will support you as you engage in decision-making with the co-parent. A mediator will frame discussions in a way that helps both of you focus on the problem at hand instead of fighting with each other. It is the mediator's job to insure that you have the information needed for good decision-making and to support you in making the choices that seem appropriate for you and your child. Most mediators are proficient in assisting people with development of specific procedures to take the guess-work out of implementing an agreement. Mediation is also a good fit for sensitive conversations that are likely to generate defensiveness.

In Conclusion ....

You now have the information you need to engage in self-centered co-parenting. You are aware of the importance of centering yourself and identifying the underlying needs that must be met to feel empowered. You are aware of the dangers of an emotional hijacking and its dysfunctional interaction with the rational thinking necessary for effective problem-solving. You are aware of the importance of focusing your attention on parenting your child instead of fighting with the other parent. You appreciate what is in your control, what influence you can have on the other parent, and some of the tools that encourage the other parent to cooperate.

Take the insights you have acquired and put them into practice. Focus on what is in your own control when the cooperation of the other parent is not what you'd like it to be. Best wishes in your endeavors to center yourself, strengthen your relationship with your child, and engage in effective problem-solving. The future looks promising.

APPENDIX ONE

Neuroscience Explains How
Our Emotions Sabotage Problem-solving

Advances in neurological research have given us insight into how the brain operates and how we can maximize it potential to help us solve problems. There are parts of the brain that are designed for this and others that can undermine and misdirect your efforts. By understanding how the brain operates, you can become aware of the signs of self-sabotage.

The limbic system is a primitive part of the human brain. It is the emotional center of the brain. The amygdala is a structure in the limbic system that stores our emotional memories and is responsible for our "fight or flight" survival responses. When feelings of fear, disgust, or apprehension are perceived by the amygdala, it triggers an unconscious automatic response designed as a reflex to protect us from situations and events that we recall as painful in our past experience. Hormones are released to provide a surge of energy that pushes us to action without conscious regard for the consequences. This is the *"Rouse – React - Reconsider"* sequence. Think of a time when you were startled by something. There was a surge of energy that interrupted your thought process and prompted you to scream or run rather than stop and inquire whether that was the best think for you to do under the circumstances. It took some time before you were calm enough to reflect on your reaction and evaluate whether it was a silly or wise decision.

The human brain is programmed to react instinctively to fear or pain. An aroused amygdala can take up to sixty minutes to calm down.

Additional painful experiences also have an impression on this emotional memory center. Over time, sequential stimulations tend to invoke stronger reactions.

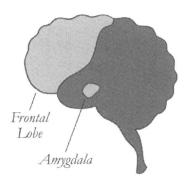

Frontal Lobe

Amygdala

The part of the brain we want to engage for problem-solving is the prefrontal cortex, which is located in the frontal lobe of the brain. It can be engaged to manage purely reactive and instinctive behavior. The working memory of the human brain is vast, which is important for problem-solving functions. When we engage this part of the brain we are executing the *"Rouse – Reflect – Proceed"* sequence. For making child-focused decisions, we definitely benefit from thinking about consequences and the best response before we act. By engaging the problem-solving capacity of the pre-frontal cortex, we avoid the sabotage of an emotional hijacking by the amygdala. Conscious decision-making engages a logical thought process that involves the entire brain. We evaluate information to check our personal biases. We seek more data to make the most informed decision possible. Our moral and cultural values guide our thoughts. We make predictions about the probable consequences - a process called rational predictability.

A significant difficulty for human brain function is that the amygdala and pre-frontal cortex have no direct connections. It takes some time and space for them to interact. You may have experienced this during a heated conversation when you could not think of the right thing to say in the moment, only to have it occur to you later. The importance of managing our emotions so our problem-thinking function can engage cannot be understated. Self-discipline and introspection are tools that are crucial for initiating the decision-making process. By becoming aware of the signs of an emotional hijacking, we have the opportunity to stop and take time to compose ourselves before proceeding with problem-solving. Creating space to think things through is a practice that you should honor both for yourself and for the co-parent.

APPENDIX TWO

When to Go to Court

Taking an uncooperative co-parent to court has its attractions. Imagine someone with authority telling the co-parent what to do, even imposing sanctions, while you sit placidly on the sidelines; then you leave the courthouse, problem solved! Few parents who go through a contested proceeding, however, see any lasting dramatic difference in the level of cooperation from the co-parent afterwards. More likely, the parenting relationship degenerates because of the adversarial nature of litigation and new resentments incurred.

Court has an appropriate role. As a parent who embraces self-centered co-parenting, you need to understanding the role and limits of the Court. The function of litigation in family law matters is to declare the legal status of family relationships, divide martial assets upon divorce, provide for support for minors and for a spouse as appropriate, oversee the best interest of minor children, and protect members of the family from abuse or neglect. The judicial system is the best resource we have for seeking redress of wrongs in a relatively peacefully manner. Litigation, however, is not always the most appropriate method for managing tenuous parenting relationships.

Separation and post-separation conflict is extremely emotional. Legal analysis avoids making decisions based on emotions or the emotional needs of litigants. A judge determines the facts of a situation based on evidence presented in an orderly and dispassionate manner. (*"There will be no display of emotion in the courtroom"* is a caution given from the bench.) A judge uses the facts to determine how the law applies to your situation. The process is highly rational. Although judges often make decisions that have emotional consequences for families, their decisions do not attempt to resolve emotions. Court is not the place to manage or resolve your feelings.

There is a timing problem when you resort to court. Its interventions are at fixed points in time. Decisions are based on circumstances that exist at the time of trial. The judge will not be "on call" to rule on future implement of the plan, to monitor how implementation is going, or to automatically sanction someone for misbehavior. This is a limitation many parents fail to comprehend when they turn to the court to fix a problem with an uncooperative parent. *"It seems like my parenting plan is just a piece of paper"* is a common lament. The Court's decision provides the ground rules for future parenting, but what happens from there on is usually up to you and the co-parent.

Returning to court for enforcement or to change a previous order means starting a new procedure, which takes time. For reasons we won't further examine here, the seemly cumbersome way in which courts operate is based on the commendable principle of "due process" guaranteed by the U.S. Constitution. In most cases a judge does not make a decision binding on parents until each parent has received notice and an opportunity to be heard in court. No one appreciates the "fairness" of a decision made by a judge based only on the input of one parent.

A consultation with an experienced family lawyer is recommended to help you understand the legal concepts that affect you and your children in your jurisdiction. Judges base their decisions on statutes and decisions in other cases (case law) that have evolved over the years to set the standards for family interactions when parents live separately. Public policy in family law has changed over time. In the nineteenth century, children had the status of property until they reached adulthood. Deference was given to the father in decision-making (married women also had limited rights). In the early twentieth century, the legal rights of women improved and gradually mothers gained preference as custodians of minor children. In the second half of the twentieth century, policy changed again. Social research pointed to the significant role that both parents play in child development. The on-going participation of both parents was recognized as laws changed to prefer shared parenting. The law in most states no longer supports a preference for a parent of a specific gender as custodian. In fact, coordination of parenting between the parents is the standard in many states.

Parents often hope that getting custody will give them sufficient power to overcome the uncooperative behavior of the co-parent. It may, however, put you at more risk for uncooperative behavior. The co-parent's perception that you have more than your fair share of power can create resentment that energizes the co-parent to go to greater lengths to undermine your authority.

Not all parenting behavior can be controlled by the court. For example, it is common for a court order to state that neither parent shall belittle the other parent when talking to the child, but as a practical matter it is almost impossible to enforce. All the sanctions the court can impose take place well after the remarks are made. The court cannot take them back. Self-centered parenting strategies seek cooperation is positive ways that decrease the rancor between parents instead of using forcing techniques that can increase defensiveness and resistance. The business model for co-parent interactions decreases the emotional intensity of the relationship. Court orders are useful in setting the terms of the business relationship but do not have the power to decree an attitude adjustment.

A principle known as "equity" holds that we must do the right thing in order to ask a court to hold the other parent to the same standard. Most courts will not overlook bad behavior by one parent when asked to enforce compliance with the court order by the other parent. For example, a parent who keeps the child from the other parent at the end of scheduled parenting time is not in a strong a position to complain about similar conduct by the other parent. A parent who faithfully observes the parenting plan is more likely to obtain the sympathetic ear of the court.

Another misconception is that a Court will impose the full extent of help and punishment you may think appropriate. In the midst of conflict, our position seems so clear and correct to us that it is easy to lose sight of other concerns. The mission of family courts is to protect the rights of children and their parents in a fair and balanced manner, without restricting or limiting legal rights any more than necessary under the circumstances. A judge is usually careful not to impose restrictions or limitations more harsh than necessary to deter inappropriate conduct. For example, a parent who is concerned about the child's welfare while under supervision of the co-parent may strongly feel that stopping the child from seeing that parent completely is for the best. Cutting off access between child and parent is one of the most extreme remedies in family law and is not undertaken lightly. Other options such as monitored visits, or assignment of a parenting coordinator, and/or counseling, will usually be ordered in preference to a no contact order.

Relying solely on a third-party decision-maker (a judge) as your go-to resource also decreases your flexibility and freedom of choice. There will be times when asking the Court to decide is your best option, but for the most part the role of the Court is ancillary to your role as parent. When you turn decision-making over to the judge, you run the risk the judge won't see it your way or may put more emphasis on issues that are not your top priority. Litigation involves a considerable investment of your time, effort and money. This is time, effort and money diverted from parenting your child. Consult a lawyer who is well versed in family law before making your decision about litigation.

It is crucial to thoughtfully weigh several questions before you resort to Court.

▶ **Is my issue one that Court can address?** Your dispute with the co-parent may hinge of matters of personal taste or conflicting but appropriate ideas about how to accomplish a parenting goal. Your personal standards of parenting, discipline, diet, or housing may vary significantly from what is deemed adequate by a judge. Unless detrimental to the child, a judge is unlikely to impose requirements beyond the basics. Negotiating these issues with the co-parent using the self-centered co-parenting techniques will be more effective.

▶ **Will a one-time decision in Court fix this?** Judges sometimes lecture parents on expected future behavior at the end of a hearing. Most of the time their words are forgotten soon after the parents leave the courthouse. A third party decision maker is helpful for setting ground rules, but that does not result in automatic buy-in. If the co-parent does not change, you may need to return to court several more times to enforce compliance. Your self-centered parenting strategies may be a better approach for gaining coopertion.

▶ **Can Court address my concern in a reasonable time frame?** A judge is not on call to hear family disputes except in the most extreme situations involving the health and welfare of your child. Court procedures require formal notice and hearings in most cases. This takes time. Family life is often lived in the moment, and a delay of months in order to deal with an issue will be frustrating. Consider other more timely options, such as mediation, to address disputes within a reasonable time frame.

▶ **Is this a good use of my resources?** Court proceedings take time, money, and divert your attention from parenting and other pursuits. Adversarial proceedings take a personal toll. Is the potential outcome likely to bring the lasting results that are worth the diversion of your resources?

▶ **Will court proceedings make things better or worse?** Court is an adversarial process. There is substantial likelihood that the dispute will intensify. The co-parent may become more adamant about the issue, more combative or more avoidant, and usually even less cooperative. The process and the after effects should be taken into consideration. Is the issue so crucial that it is worth undertaking the risks inherent in adversarial proceedings? Your self-centered parenting skills may be more helpful to soften the position of the other parent on the issue, rather than hardening it.

▶ **What is the risk of an adverse ruling?** Turning decision-making over to a third party always involves some risk. Be sure to seek professional advice on the risks you are facing when seeking redress in court. It is difficult to see the other side of an issue when we have strong feelings. Resist the impulse to discount the position of the co-parent. The co-parent will also be advocating their views in court. If you think your issue is a "slam dunk" check it out first with your lawyer.

APPENDIX 3
The Child's Bill of Rights

1. I am a unique and valued human being with my own personality, thoughts, and feelings.

2. I am entitled to be loved and have family members make decisions about my welfare based on my best interest.

3. I am entitled to develop an appropriate positive relationship with each parent who lives separately without interference.

4. I am entitled to attention to my physical needs for food, shelter, clothing, and appropriate healthcare/dental care.

5. I am entitled to have my physical needs meet by both parents without interference.

6. I am entitled to form appropriate emotional attachments with each parent, members of my family, and my extended family.

7. I am entitled to a loving and nurturing parental relationship that provides me with the freedom to discuss my fears and concerns in a supportive and non-judgmental way.

8. I am entitled to a childhood free from feelings of blame, disloyalty, or betrayal arising from the nature of my relationship with a parent or co-parent.

9. I am entitled to an honest relationship with all family members and I should not be asked to take sides or to be disloyal to either parent or any other family member.

10. I have legal rights even though I am a child and I should not be used as a bargaining chip in disputes between my co-parents.

APPENDIX 4

Reducing Intimacy

An emotionally charged relationship is the fast lane to disaster when you are dealing with your child's parent who lives separately. When we are emotionally charged, our decisions are reactive instead of deliberate. The rush to fight or flee robs us of the will-power to slow down and think things out. Besides the techniques we offer for slowing down an emotionally reactive process, the best thing you can do for yourself is to change the nature of your relationship with the other parent to one that is less intimate and intense.

This graph represents the variety of human relationships.

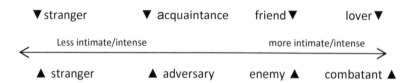

The intense end of the relationship scale is shared by positive and negative intimate relationships. The most intense and intimate positive relationship is that of lovers. When we stop being in love we do not stop having feelings. In fact, because of the value and promise we once saw in the relationship, our feelings are still engaged but in a negative way. People in active combat are as intimately and intensely entwined as people in love. People don't put everything at stake, including their child, when they are in a less intense relationship.

Where are you on the intimacy scale?

LOWER INTIMACY
(focus on parenting)

HIGHER INTIMACY
(focus on former partner)

Does not ask about or try to interfere in co-parent's personal life
O *I do this*   O *Co-parent does this*

Overly interested in co-parent's personal life, especially dating
O *I do this*   O *Co-parent does this*

Does not ask child for information about co-parent's personal life
O *I do this*   O *Co-parent does this*

Asks child about the co-parent's personal life and activities
O *I do this*   O *Co-parent does this*

Is willing to confirm facts with co-parent before reaching a conclusion
O *I do this*   O *Co-parent does this*

Jumps to negative conclusions about co-parent's motives
O *I do this*   O *Co-parent does this*

Is respectful/business-like

O *I do this*   O *Co-parent does this*

Is disrespectful, angry, mean-spirited or sarcastic
O *I do this*   O *Co-parent does this*

More focused on good decision-making and best outcomes for child than fighting with co-parent
O *I do this*   O *Co-parent does this*

More interested in proving former partner wrong that making good decisions for child
O *I do this*   O *Co-parent does this*

Conversations stay focused on child and parenting decision-making
O *I do this*   O *Co-parent does this*

Conversations bring up hard feelings, accusations and blaming
O *I do this*   O *Co-parent does this*

Willing to conduct communications necessary for caring for child
O *I do this*   O *Co-parent does this*

Avoids co-parent by refusing to answer calls, emails or texts
O *I do this*   O *Co-parent does this*

Recognizes autonomy of co-parent, focuses on own responsibility
O *I do this*   O *Co-parent does this*

Contacts co-parent in order to criticize, blame, demand action
O *I do this*   O *Co-parent does this*

Negative intimacy can lead to an addictive pattern of interactions that are stressful and heightens anxiety. Negative devaluation distorts a parent's insight into the motivations of the other parent. It prevents a parent from acknowledging good ideas or giving the co-parent any credit for positive behavior.

When one of you decides the relationship is over, it's healthy to reduce the intensity of the relationship. How far you need to dial back depends on the wishes of each of you to stay engaged. We feel somewhat attached to acquaintances and business or social contacts, but the relationship is courteous and at arm's length. The intensity and intimacy level rises as people become our friends. Some parents living separately do well as friends, although they have usually gone through a period of reducing the intimacy of the relationship over time. If you are in an intense relationship now, it may be best to dial back to acquaintances for now. There may be a desire to make your child's other parent a stranger, but that option is not available to you as long as your child is a minor. The parent-child relationship comes with responsibilities to honor your child's legal rights to care, support and access to other resources from *both* parents.

How to reduce intimacy in 4 steps

Step One: Re-labeling
Stop thinking of your child's other co-parent in the former role they occupied in your life. That person is no longer your partner or spouse. Don't refer to them as your "ex." Use a neutral terms such as co-parent, my child's other parent, etc. The use of a less emotional label will help you think of them in less intimate terms.

Step Two: Business role.
Try to come to terms with the fact that your child's other parent still has a role, though diminished, in your life. Think of him or her as an acquaintance or business contact that is a resource for your child. Try not to put any expectations on this role. You can't make the co-parent assume a role or responsibilities you want. The other parent will be involved to the extent it makes sense to him or her. Note, however, that as a self-centered co-parent you can exert influence on the other parent to become more cooperative.

Step Three: Think in terms of business transactions.

Don't expect any favors. Since the relationship has changed, the co-parent no longer has to please you. From now on, think of all interactions as business transactions. Focus on staying in the "profitable" range: put enough effort into interactions that will achieve more benefit than the effort required to achieve cooperation.

Step Four: Stay focused.

Avoid social engagement with the co-parent until you feel you can handle it without an emotional challenge.   If conflict is recurrent, limit your interactions for now to ones required to conduct business for your child, such as exchanges of the child or meeting at a parent-teacher conference. Pre-plan the interactions you need to have with co-parent. Decide what to accomplish for your child during this interaction. Commit to staying focused on your goal for your child. Sense when emotions become overwhelming and risk pulling you off task. Take a break if necessary. Don't feel compelled to make snap decisions in the moment.

Moving to a business relationship

In business you want to perform in the profitable range. Over-doing it raises expenses unnecessarily and under-performing costs you customers, increasing losses.   Commit to doing what it takes to conduct your parenting business profitably.

1.   Identify the co-parent in the new role. Stop thinking about the other parents as a former partner or ex-spouse.

2.   Adopt a problem-solving mindset. Seeing yourself as a victim is disempowering and does not achieve results for your child.

3.   Frame issues around what is best for your child, not your emotional reaction.   Your child is the "product" of your business. Protect and perfect it.

4. Provide appropriate information to the co-parent even when the co-parent doesn't reciprocate.

5. Ask for feedback. You can listen without agreeing. Respect the fact that the co-parent is entitled to have a point of view too. You need to know what it is, not just assume or guess at it. Acknowledging the co-parent's concerns is invaluable for building the rapport and respect necessary for the two-way communication required for productive negotiation.

6. Return calls and respond to requests. Be courteous even if you are not feeling it. Keep your inner thoughts to yourself. Filter what to say in order to address the issue, not your feelings about the issue.

7. Change an *Either/Or* negotiation orientation to a *Both/And* orientation. You have your child in common and your child is best served when you jointly pursue finding the best solution to a problem. The solution you both agree upon is more workable and enduring than any concession obtained under duress.

8. Be willing to negotiate to achieve your priorities. Remember that it takes two to reach an agreement and that some of the co-parent's needs and priorities must be addressed in any agreement too. There are often opportunities to meet priorities of both parents at the same time without giving in on fundamental concerns.

APPENDIX 5

Identify Your Emotions and Needs

Our emotions are indicators of our unmet needs. Awareness of a general feeling, such as "I'm mad" needs to be identified as a specific emotion or emotions. Think about what this emotion is stirring up. What is not being taken care of? What do you wish you had more of? This is the need that you are trying to satisfy.

Alarm	Frustration	Misery
Agitation	Fulfillment	Nervousness
Anger	Fury	Numbness
Anxiety	Gloom	Panic
Apathy	Guilt	Puzzlement
Bewilderment	Happiness	Reassurance
Bitterness	Helplessness	Relief
Boredom	Hesitance	Resentment
Concern	Horror	Sadness
Confusion	Hostility	Shock
Depression	Impatience	Skepticism
Disappointment	Indifference	Sorrow
Discomfort	Irritation	Terror
Disgust	Jealousy	Vexation
Fatigue	Joy	Vindication
Fear	Loneliness	Weariness
Fright	Love	Worry

For a comprehensive list of specific emotions connected to needs met and unmet, consult *Non-Violent Communication, A Language of Compassion*, Marshall Rosenberg, Puddledancer Press (1999)

APPENDIX 6

Role of Thinking Preferences

How preferences affect our communication style

Our thinking preferences impact how we process information and what we perceive as most important in interactions with others. Thinking preference frames are based on decades of research into how our brain works and how we relate to others. Roger Sperry's experiments identified the specialization of the left and right hemispheres of the human brain and how they interact. Ned Herrmann identified four thinking preference styles: two that are left brain dominant (language and rational thinking) and two styles that are right brain dominant (music, imagery and creativity). We use all four thinking styles to some extent but not many people have a perfect balance of all four thinking styles. Most people have a preference for one or two particular thinking styles. Researchers have also found that people feel most comfortable when their thinking preference is compatible with the thinking style required by the work or their personal life. To determine your own thinking preferences you can find assessment surveys, like the Hermann Brain Dominance Instrument, online.

Awareness of your thinking preferences is valuable in figuring out how to interact with people with different thinking preferences. When you and the co-parent have different thinking preferences, knowing where they put emphasis and priority is valuable in molding you communications in ways to which they are most receptive.

Thinking Preference Quadrants

Analyst
(left brain)

Enjoys looking at an idea or problem from all angles and evaluating what is best to do. Can get bogged down in ruminating.

Frustrated by dreaming that does not sync with reality. May be annoyed by over-emphasis on steps and procedures.

Processing information and reaching a conclusion takes priority over concerns about relationships.

Visionary
(right brain)

Enjoys thinking about the big picture and dreaming of how things might be. Visioning is energizing but unproductive without organization and planning.

Finds analysis that examines and criticizes vision threatening. Feels bogged down when asked to flesh out the details.

Vision takes priority over concerns about relationships.

Taskmaster
(left brain)

Enjoys implementing and successfully completing tasks. Can be bogged down in the details of planning.

Annoyed by big picture thinking that doesn't come down to earth. Frustrated by analysis that doesn't hone in on the steps and procedures needed to complete the task.

Task completion takes priority over concerns about relationships.

Socialite
(right brain)

Relationships with others are of primary importance. Enjoys being a team member and positive interaction with others. Expects others to take their feelings into account and put this above other priorities.

Frustrated by Analysts, Visionaries, and Disciplinarians. Sees their priorities as means to forming and maintaining relationships, not as ends in themselves.

Effective communications

▶ **Analyst:** Needs information and time to evaluate data before reaching a decision. An analyst tends to discount new ideas until proven and relates more easily to a Taskmaster than a Visionary or Socialite.

▶ **Visionary:** Enjoys brainstorming, but needs feedback and encouragement to refine the vision. A visionary is more receptive to questions about how the idea will work than to criticism of the idea. A Visionary finds it most difficult to work with the Taskmaster, who is perceived as getting bogged down in the details rather than being energized by the vision.

▶ **Taskmaster:** Needs to process the details for implementation in order to feel comfortable with an idea. A Taskmaster is easily frustrated by all other thinking preferences because they do not give procedures and rules enough priority. A Taskmaster needs to have information and feedback that provides specifics about how things will work and who is responsible for the required tasks.

▶ **Socialite:** Needs positive and respectful interactions, and honors reciprocity (treat me well, I'll treat you well). Wants to cooperate with good ideas, but is not as particular about the details as the relationship between people. A socialite needs positive and respectful interaction along with ideas and details. Discounting a positive social interaction makes them fearful or suspicious.

APPENDIX 7

The Use of Nudges

Nudge, a book published in 2008 by Richard Thaler and Cass Sunstein, focused attention on the science of "choice architecture." They reported on the trends in business, social services, and government to "nudge" people toward decisions that will improve their lives. They defined a nudge as a technique "that alters people's behavior in a predictable way without forbidding any options or significantly changing their incentives." They also discussed the reasons why prohibitions and mandates are ineffective and even counter-productive.

Nudges are often used by car manufacturers. The reputation of their product is enhanced when they help owners of their cars to make good decisions about safe operation of the vehicle. Some nudges are defaults, such as headlights coming on automatically when the windshield wipers are activated. A low cost nudge is the plastic loop that keeps the fuel cap attached to the gas tank. In the past, a driver had to remove the gas cap when filling the tank and it was often set somewhere else until fueling was finished. It was easy to forget to put the cap back on the tank. Without the cap, fuel would evaporate or spill out of the tank, a costly and dangerous mistake. By attaching the fuel cap to the tank with a plastic loop, the cap remains in sight. The driver is nudged to replace the cap. A good nudge presents a good choice and doesn't create resistance by making it a mandate. A car owner's resistance to the fuel cap nudge is decreased because the owner is free to make the choice to cut the plastic cord without changing the vehicle's performance.

Nudges are particularly valuable when they educate us about our options. More information can improve the quality of choosing. For example, making the minimum payment on a credit card each month seems attractive because it increases your disposable income. The decision to pay the minimum, however, does not take future consequences into consideration. The credit card company provides information on your statement about the actual cost of credit over time if only the minimum payment is made. This is a nudge toward thinking about future costs and whether you may want to reduce your cost of credit. You may still pay the monthly minimum, or you may choose to pay something more, based on your needs and preference. This is the beauty of nudges. They promote better decision-making with information that helps us think about our decision in a larger context. Nudges also promote more consistent choosing since it prompts us to processing the reasons for our choice. When every future credit card statement is received the decision to pay a little more is easier to act on since we have previously processed information about our best choice.

Nudges are also effective when the time of making a choice and the time of noticing the impact are separated. When there is no timely link between choice and consequence, it is easy to overlook the future consequences. Nudges help motivate us to do those things on a regular basis in order to avoiding future unpleasant consequences. Without a nudge to brush teeth before bedtime your child may forget to do so. Your child may not connect daily brushing with the consequences on dental hygiene until the next dental checkup. A nudge to brush teeth daily can further be enhanced by providing an attractive tooth brush and tooth paste, and praising the child for doing a good job.

A nudge should be designed with the lowest possible administrative costs. Here is a simple example of the range of costs involved in a nudge for your child to make healthier food choices. You could ban all sweets and desserts in your house to prohibit your child from making poor choices, but prohibitions have high administrative costs.

You also suffer because sweets and desserts aren't available to you either. If you hide sweets, your child is tempted to get some on the sly. If your child is aware you are hiding sweets you are likely to be the recipient of whining and complaining and begging for sweets, which saps your energy and will power to enforce your no sweets policy. Prohibitions have limited value because they don't teach your child how to make better choices at school or the homes of friends. A better nudge provides some options that empower your child to make good choices. You could include fruits and other alternatives to sweets at home. By placing them where they are more accessible than sweets, you are nudging your child to consume the healthier snacks. You could also make a house rule that allows the child to have a special treat after a predetermined number of more health treats. This is a habit the child can internalize and follow outside your home. The child feels less deprived, you feel better that the child has a healthier diet, and your child is learning how to make more desirable choices.

APPENDIX 8

Picking an Appropriate Negotiation Style

Personality and habit steers our preference for one or two ways of negotiating. Flexibility is necessary to pick the most appropriate negotiation style for the situation. Negotiation strategies range from very uncooperative and non-assertive to very cooperative and assertive.

Fight Satisfy my needs only	**Build a Bridge** Satisfy some of the needs of both	**Team Up** Maximize satisfying needs of both
Flee No needs satisfied		**Oblige** Satisfy needs of others

A s s e r t i v e →

Cooperative →

Fight and Flee are negotiating styles based in emotional reactivity. Neither is very cooperative. Fleeing is non-assertive and avoids addressing a conflict; therefore, no one's needs are satisfied.

Fighting is non-cooperative but very assertive. Negotiation is combative and focused on satisfying one's own needs without regard to the needs of others. This is the *Either/Or* orientation for problem solving. A "win" depends on having the power to prevail over others. Winning at the expense of others provokes resentment and revenge. In the fight mode parents see each other as opponents. They are more susceptible to discounting whatever the other parent says or proposes (negative devaluation*)*. This is an emotional reaction to the person instead of an objective assessment of the proposal.

Bridge building, teaming up, and obliging negotiation strategies are more cooperative. Bridge building decreases the risk of loss by seeking to satisfy the highest priority needs of both sides. Each person gives up on a total individual win to reduce risk and secure an outcome each can live with. Obliging is even more cooperative and less assertive. It is a good strategy for building social capital when agreeing will cost you little but is valuable to the other side. It sets the tone for reciprocity. Teaming up is the negotiation frame that is both assertive and cooperative. Each side seeks to maximize their own satisfaction while also seeking solutions that satisfy the needs of the other side. This is the *Both/And* orientation for problem solving.

Most parenting issues can be addressed by using any of the five negotiation styles. The trick is to select the one that is most likely to result in agreement you can tolerate under the circumstances. Consider a decision about orthodontia for your child. Avoiding may be the preferred choice when the child's need for braces is still speculative and far in the future. When the likelihood of orthodontia is great, it is beneficial to address the future need for orthodontic services now. Terms of the parenting plan can include who will make the selection of the provider, who will arrange for services, provisions for insurance to cover part of the cost, and what proportion of the out-of-pocket cost will be paid by each parent. Teaming up to solve this problem is most effective when both parents acknowledge that braces are necessary and they are willing to find acceptable ways to manage the cost. Obliging may play a part in the negotiation, for instance, if one parent already carries dental insurance and is willing to commit to maintain it throughout orthodontia services. When the co-parent does not agree on the necessity of treatment, is worried about the cost, or resists making the decision, you could resort to the fight mode to put terms in place. Litigation is a variety of the fight mode, where a third-party (judge) makes the decision on the details. Be prepared, however, that the terms set forth in a court order require future performance and it may take additional effort to enforce performance. It is also worth weighing the risk of an adverse or unpalatable decision in court. The higher the risk, the more attractive bridge building becomes. Parents approach bridge building by trying to limit losses and retain some satisfaction with the outcome.

Parents express more satisfaction when they negotiate their parenting plan as a whole instead of piece by piece. Each item to be addressed in the parenting plan can be thought of as a pizza. By putting all the pizzas out on the negotiating table, the parents create a pizza buffet from which they can select what makes most sense to them. Your plan is more satisfying and more likely to last when each parent feels they were able to address as many of their needs and concerns as possible.

In addition to selecting a negotiation style, there is a variety of bargaining techniques that are effective in helping parents reach agreement. Here are some of the most common techniques:

● *Prioritizing* – Each parent makes choices according to their most important needs and concerns. This works well when only the most important priorities can be accommodated, such as selection of a limited number of extracurricular activities for the child.

● *Alternating choices* – Each parent has an opportunity to choose according their own priorities while alternating choices between one parent and then the other. This can work well, for example, in selection of parenting time on holidays.

● *Equitable choosing* – When a resource is finite, the suspicion that one parent is overreaching is diminished when one parent divides the resource into equal parts and the other parent has first pick. This works well, for example in distributing equal amounts of parenting time, such as specific periods for summer vacation.

- *Overlapping interests* – Parents may find some interests, though different, are still compatible. This may work well, for example, in determining how the child's birthday will be celebrated. Both parents are interested in celebrating with the child, but one parent prefers celebrating on the exact birthday, while the other parent is satisfied fine with celebrating on a weekend nearest the birthday.

- *Tradeoffs* – This is a means of gaining support for something that is more important to you by agreeing to accommodate something that is more important to the other parent. For example a parent is usually willing to let the other parent have Father's Day if more interested in celebrating Mother's Day.

To boost your satisfaction with the outcome of a negotiation, consider using a negotiation professional. Data the author collected over a fifteen year period demonstrates that co-parents who engage in mediation decrease by fifty percent the likelihood they will take a future parenting dispute to court. The mediation process helps parents gain insight and confidence that they can negotiate more effectively. Mediators are proficient at identifying the underlying needs that people want to fill in order to get to yes. They reframe the discussion in a way that supports all participants in the discussion to raise their concerns. Mediation seeks a consensual outcome that supports free choice. The process builds the commitment of each participant to the final resolution and increases the probability that their agreement will last, certainly much longer than imposed solutions.

APPENDIX 9

RECOMMENDED READING

The Co-Parenting Survival Guide: Letting Go of Conflict after a Difficult Divorce, Elizabeth S. Thayer & Jeffrey Zimmerman, New Harbinger Publications (2001)

Custody Chaos, Personal Peace: Sharing Custody with a Ex Who Drives You Crazy, Jeffrey P. Wittman, PhD, Berkley Publishing Group (2001)

Difficult Conversations: How to Discuss What Matters Most, D. Stone, B. Patton, S. Heen, Penguin Books (1999)

Getting to Yes with Yourself (and Other Worthy Opponents), William Ury, U.S. Harper One (2015)

Joint Custody with a Jerk, J. Ross and J. Corcoran, St. Martin's Press (2011 edition)

Non-Violent Communication, A Language of Compassion, Marshall Rosenberg, Puddledancer Press (1999).

Nudge: Improving Decisions About Health, Wealth and Happiness, Richard H. Thaler and Cass R. Sunstein, Yale University Press (2008)

Taking the War Out of Our Words: The Art of Powerful Non-Defensive Communication, Sharon Strand Ellison, Wyatt-McKenzie Publishing Inc. (2008)

Made in the USA
Columbia, SC
18 August 2019